EVALUATING

SOCIAL DEVELOPMENT

PROJECTS

Edited by
David Marsden and Peter Oakley

Development Guidelines No. 5
(Series editor, Brian Pratt)

OXFAM

British Library Cataloguing in Publication Data
Evaluating social development projects. — (Development
guidelines;no.5).
   1. Developing countries. Social development. Projects. Assessment
   I. Marsden, David II. Oakley, Peter III. Series
   361.61091724

ISBN 0-85598-146-6 hbk
ISBN 0-85598-147-4 pbk

Published by Oxfam, 274 Banbury Road, Oxford OX2 7DZ
Designed by Oxfam Design Studio/Opus Design Group
Printed by Oxfam Print Unit
Typeset in 11 pt. Garamond

Contents

Foreword

Evaluating Social Development Projects is different from earlier books in Oxfam's *Development Guidelines* series. Each previous book has provided a summary of practical experience in the field of evaluation, with accompanying guidelines for practitioners. The present volume aims to take forward debate about the difficult issues relating to the evaluation of social development, in the knowledge that there are still unanswered questions, and a need for more direct practical application of the concepts presented here.

Oxfam has been concerned to improve the methods of evaluating social development work since the 1970s. The move towards development in terms of empowerment, social democracy, and popular participation required an approach to evaluation which went far beyond the traditional and limited methods which stressed simple quantitative indices of activity, impact, results, and achievements. In the 1970s Oxfam supported the work of Marie-Therese Feuerstein with women's groups in Honduras, which helped to clarify many of the issues and benefits of participatory evaluation. Later, support was given to the work of Peter Oakley and David Winder in Latin America and India, which sought to clarify the criteria and indices for use in the evaluation of social development. Our support for the conference held in Swansea in 1989 upon which this present book is based reflects our belief that the debate has not ended, and that there is a need for further clarification of concepts and sharing of experiences in this area.

It is hoped that this book will stimulate more debate and action in this important area. One major step will be to 'operationalise' some of the concepts elaborated here. Further evaluations of social development programmes will create a wider base of experience from which to refine our knowledge of such evaluations. Eventually it should be possible to produce a 'state of the art' volume on the evaluation of social development which will provide direct guidance to evaluators, without losing the flexibility which is the hallmark of good social development.

Brian Pratt
Oxford
August 1990

Acknowledgements

This book is based upon the proceedings of an international conference which we convened on the Evaluation of Social Development Projects in the Third World, held at the Centre for Development Studies, University College, Swansea, 19-22 September, 1989. We are most grateful to the following organisations which gave us financial support: Action Aid, the Catholic Fund for Overseas Development (CAFOD), Cebemo (Netherlands), the UN Food and Agriculture Organisation (FAO), Misereor (Germany), the Overseas Development Administration (ODA), and Oxfam. This generous support allowed us not only to keep the cost of the conference to a minimum, but also to offer ten bursaries to Third World students to attend.

The conference went smoothly and certainly gave us few headaches, thanks to the excellent support we received. Denise Johns, as Secretary to the conference, was wonderful; Jenny Marr and Anette Arndt gave splendid support during the week of the conference. Our thanks also to David Brown, Patricia Goldey, Brian Pratt, Peter Sollis, and Geoff Wood for serving as rapporteurs and for providing us with prompt notes, and to the Centre for Development Studies, under the direction of Professor Alan Rew, for hosting the conference and supporting us throughout; and to Ana Toni and Anette Arndt for very prompt research assistance in preparing this book.

Particular thanks to Heinz Knuvener (Misereor), Tony Fernandes (Cebemo), and Brian Pratt (Oxfam), who joined us in a planning committee to help prepare for the conference, and gave us great support and encouragement throughout.

Finally, our sincere thanks to the 80 or so participants for helping to create what we believe turned out to be a warm, friendly and stimulating conference.

David Marsden
Peter Oakley
June 1990

Introduction

Background

A four-day conference was held at the Centre for Development Studies, University College of Swansea in Wales in September 1989. It brought together a variety of individuals and institutions to address the issue of the evaluation of social development projects which focus on *process* rather than on *product* and which are thus difficult to evaluate using conventional methodologies. As Bryant and White observe:

> It is not an easy matter to examine whether the goals of development are being met when those goals include the improvement of qualitative characteristics such as capacity which cannot be directly observed. (Bryant and White 1982)

The goals of many social development projects and programmes involve such things as the development of indigenous sustainable capacity, the promotion of participation, the awakening of consciousness, and the encouragement of self-reliant strategies. How are these to be measured? What are the purposes of evaluations of these sorts of projects? Who does the evaluations and when is the best time to undertake them? Are evaluations of these types of projects essentially different from those of more conventional infrastructural projects? Is it possible to clarify objectives in more detail?

Because we are dealing with development strategies which are rather different from those which emphasise production, new techniques and new methods need to be devised. We are dealing with a changing set of relationships between actors involved in the development process and a changing scientific and social environment, where the old orthodoxies associated with Northern liberal scientific principles of economic development, backed by objective analysis, no longer hold. We are negotiating new ways in which value can be analysed, and new methodologies which will provide more appropriate ways of understanding the effectiveness of interventions in the name of social development.

The conference was searching not only for more appropriate methods and techniques to assess the achievements of such projects, but also for a new understanding of what evaluation might mean. This struggle for a new understanding takes place against a background of changing views about the nature of the development task; of a recognition of the relativity of

Western scientific explanations and thus of the claims of Western science to objectivity; of an emerging global order and the recognition of the importance of different value systems in the elaboration of appropriate development styles; and of a recognition of the importance of building sustainability, equity and solidarity into development initiatives. These have fundamental implications for relationships between donors and recipients in a renegotiated relationship between members of the 'project community'.

The initial overview papers by David Marsden and Peter Oakley attempted to sketch out the meaning of social development and the current state of the art in terms of the evaluation of social development projects and programmes respectively. David Marsden's paper provided an historical overview of changes that have led to current thinking in the field of social development. Peter Oakley's paper provided an overview of the current state of the art in thinking about evaluation, and presented some of the challenges which are likely to face those trying to re-formulate strategies towards evaluation.

The conference addressed four separate themes:

— The elaboration of more appropriate qualitative indicators to be used in evaluation.
— Methodologies for the evaluation of social development projects and programmes.
— Partnership in evaluation, and the changing nature of relationships between funders/donors and recipients.
— The role and position of the evaluator.

The definition of social development which the conference used as a basis for discussion was contained in the introductory leaflet sent out to invite people to participate. It emphasises the need to focus on the development and maintenance of organisations of the poor in order to enhance sustainable and equitable development and ensure increased access to available resources. This notion of development cannot be seen as merely something that is confined to the poor South; social development is also about the development of the rich North in an evolving global partnership. The elaboration of a new economic and social order cannot merely be about devising more appropriate forms of intervention in the South. It must also be about changing appreciations of the nature of the development task in the North as well. While this definition is not meant to be all-inclusive or definitive, it does offer an indication of the direction the conference wished to take.

The conference was sponsored by a number of different agencies including Misereor (West Germany), Cebemo (The Netherlands), Oxfam (UK), the Overseas Development Administration of the UK government, the Intermediate Technology Development Group (UK), the Food and Agriculture Organisation (FAO), Action Aid (UK), and the journal *Community Development*. This sponsorship allowed the participation of a significant group of people from outside Europe, and also provided bursaries for study fellows resident in the UK and the Netherlands to attend. Some 80 people were directly involved, and all continents of the world were represented. The conference was characterised by a significantly high level of engagement and participation, reflected in the large numbers of contributions tabled for discussion, and reflecting the current importance attached to the evaluation of these increasingly central types of projects and programmes.

The conference provided an opportunity for major non-governmental organisations (NGOs) in Europe to share experiences in a field which is currently receiving considerable attention. People want to know how to measure the progress of projects in which they have invested resources and from which there has been very little documented information about achievement — to assess whether resources are being channelled in the most appropriate ways. In addition to this, at the heart of the discussions was the search for a more appropriate form of intervention which puts *people* at the centre of the stage.

As well as non-government organisations of the North, governmental and multilateral agencies, such as DANIDA, the FAO, the International Labour Organisation (ILO), and the World Bank, were represented, together with partners from the South and a number of British academics. With the Single European Market in mind, the conference provided an opportunity to consider the issue of European-ness, and how it might influence approaches to working in the Third World.

The conference had its origins in meetings between a small number of people at a series of symposia jointly organised by the German Foundation for International Development (DSE), the German Ministry for Technical Cooperation, and the FAO. It was rooted in concerns to grapple with the tricky issues of *empowerment, capacity-building, participation* and *grassroots development.* These were perceived as essential for any sustainable development strategy. It was felt that many of the more productive advances were likely to be taking place within the non-governmental sector, because of its perceived ability to innovate and experiment in ways in which governments, and agencies operating in terms of governments, perhaps could not.

Thematic papers

The four major themes of the conference were introduced by four invited speakers. Anisur Rahman focused on qualitative indicators in a search for more appropriate means whereby meaningful development might be measured. Ignacio Garaycochea addressed the issue of appropriate methodologies for the evaluation of social development projects and programmes. Rajesh Tandon examined the issue of partnership in evaluations, and the dilemmas associated with cooperation between donors and recipients. And Delle Tiongson-Brouwers focused on the dilemmas associated with the role of the evaluator. After the presentation of these four papers and reflections on them and on the two introductory papers, the conference divided into smaller groups to work through the issues raised. The results of these discussions were brought back to a plenary session on the last morning of the conference.

The search for more appropriate indicators

Anisur Rahman argued that indicators should be developed in the context of the individual project's or programme's actual objectives. Central attention should be given to the local people's culture in the formulation of indicators. He introduced the important concept of the *project community*, which includes all concerned with the implementation of the project or programme. He emphasised that the evaluation experience should be a *learning process* for all in the project community. In trying to identify more appropriate indicators, it was suggested that measurement of access to basic needs was not necessarily as important as the measurement of human dignity, mutual respect, and solidarity. Education, rather than material benefits, might be the most important gain in the people's own assessment of what they had achieved through organisation.

In addressing the question of who assesses development, Rahman focused on the promoters of social development. How far should we, as outsiders, impose parameters on the local people? The process of *empowering* and *enabling* must be an essential dimension of social development and must be undertaken by the people themselves. Three elements of empowerment were briefly dealt with. These were the organisation of the disadvantaged, the development of social awareness which enabled the disadvantaged to develop a sense of equality with the formally 'educated' classes of society, and the encouragement of self-reliance. An educational process which focused on these three elements should question seriously the modes by which literacy, as an important tool in dealing with public and other agencies, is acquired. Literacy should not be another means by which the poor surrender their independence to the literate elites. With

4

these three basic elements assured, the process of organic development can proceed through the development of creativity, of appropriate institutions, of collective management, and through solidarity.

Specific attention should be given to ensuring that women are able to assert their own points of view, and the importance of popular or organic knowledge should be stressed. The development of knowledge which is more immediately relevant for self-sustaining development will be an important indicator of the success of social development projects and programmes. This implies a greater recognition of the importance of cultural diversity and the legitimacy of people's assertions of their cultural identities.

More appropriate methodologies

Ignacio Garaycochea was asked to explore the issue of appropriate methodologies for the evaluation of social development projects and programmes. He argued that the different interpretations of what social development means will have a significant impact on the design of methodologies to measure their effectiveness. These would vary according to whether one thought of social development in terms of *conscientisation*, *popular education*, or *empowerment*. Different understandings lead to different methodologies being adopted. Social development must be seen as essentially a *process*, and evaluation must thus be seen as an organic part of that process. Within that process there will be a continual negotiation of objectives, and the idea of setting particularly distinct pre-determined objectives thus has little value. Negotiating objectives is part of the learning process. In 'process' projects, however, it is not possible to contrast 'before' and 'after' situations, because of the usual absence of base-line data, and also because of its minimal relevance in projects of this kind. Evaluation is then about selecting elements which best describe the project.

If projects are to continue receiving funding, then there must be reliable evidence of positive changes. Numbers provide 'objective/reliable' statements and can always be assembled. It is possible to measure non-tangible objectives in some way. The debate should not be between quantitative and qualitative measurements. You can put a number on anything if you wish to; it is the interpretation of that number which is important.

This interpretation must be part of the process, and, in order to minimise subjectivity, it must include as many different perspectives as possible. The evaluation process itself should provide an element of contrast, so that people can gain distance from their immediate practice, and in so doing achieve greater understanding of the processes in which they are engaged.

The changing relationship between donors and recipients

Rajesh Tandon tackled the issue of relationships between donors and recipients in the evaluation of social development projects and programmes. His paper, entitled 'Partnership in Social Development Evaluation', began from the fundamental assumption that evaluation is an educational intervention — a learning opportunity for the project community; rather than being seen as judgemental, evaluations should be viewed as *developmental*. Social development evaluation must enhance confidence and capacity, and thus echo the empowering principles central to most social development interventions. It must link an understanding of the past with a vision of the future — to clarify 'the mission' through restatement or reformulation.

If evaluations are carried out with these principles, then there are fundamental issues for partnership; partnership becomes inextricably linked to a particular philosophy of development.

> If our philosophy of development puts people in the centre, if we believe that development cannot be done from outside but is sustained and elaborated by the group of people on their own, if we believe that development is not merely a series of events but processes, organisations, people spread over long periods of time, then we have to see that partnership is fundamental to any such social development effort.

Thus any sustainable, long-term, and self-reliant development strategy requires the construction and maintenance of strong partnerships across like-minded constituencies within the project community. Partnership across <u>unequal constituencies</u> is extremely difficult to construct, and in order for attempts to bridge this gap between levels within the project community, there must be some notion of *mutuality*. Partnership is not simply intellectual camaraderie, but is fundamental to notions of solidarity within and between constituencies struggling with the development process.

In the evaluation, different constituencies within the project community may feel more at home with the use of different forms of evaluation methods. It is necessary to understand these different methods and the parameters of their use, in order to encourage reflection and learning from the educative process of evaluation. In selecting the most appropriate methods to facilitate partnership, it is essential to know who regulates the evaluation process, who benefits from the evaluation, and who utilises the information derived from the evaluation. The essence of partnership is to ensure that evaluations are cooperative and critical, rather than instrumental and technocratic.

Issues raised in the discussion groups and plenary sessions

Given the great variety of interests represented at the conference, it is a difficult task to capture the many different ideas raised in the plenary sessions as well as in the workshop groups. Indeed the spirit of the conference would militate against such capture, if it were to be seen as a way of foreclosing on the debate. At the risk of misrepresenting what individuals and spokespeople contributed, we can perhaps identify a series of common themes and a set of questions that cry out for further discussion.

Evaluations as learning experiences

Major stress was given to the fact that evaluations should be fundamentally reoriented to become learning experiences for all involved in the evaluation process; their purpose should be developmental rather than judgemental. In line with an approach that is process-oriented rather than product-oriented, evaluations should not be seen as separate discrete activities; they should pervade the process of development itself and become an integral part of the continuous reorientation and internal examination of objectives required of process projects. As such, the chronological distinctions that have traditionally separated evaluations from appraisals and from monitoring exercises are necessarily blurred. The exercise is a continual and a participatory one. Quite different attitudes to evaluation need to be cultivated, and this requires a rethinking of the role of the external, objective, outsider who traditionally is given the responsibility for evaluations.

Re-alignment between donor and beneficiary

With a re-oriented approach to evaluation, the issues of accountability, the formulation of objectives, and the ways in which costs and benefits are measured need also to be re-thought. If evaluation is to be truly participative, if people are really to be put at the centre of the process, then there must be a fundamental re-alignment of the relationship between donor agency and beneficiary.

Evaluations take place in a field of tension, where the conflicting interests of the different members of the project community are brought together. It is important to recognise these differing interests and to work through a methodology which can provide a forum where these might be publicly dealt with and which can produce something which is less hierarchical and less judgemental than currently obtains. Partnership means that donors and recipients move towards a position of mutuality in which reciprocal evaluations might take place, in order to strengthen solidarity between those who provide financial resources and those who provide legitimacy for the disbursement of those resources. This trust and mutual respect must not, however, remain unrecorded on the common assumption that people who operate on the basis of trust need not formalise that relationship. For a variety of reasons — more successful inter-agency communication, public accountability, and the need to ensure that an institutional memory develops — there is a need for effective documentation. While trust and mutual respect are central to this process, it is very difficult to achieve, given the apparent asymmetry in the relationship between Northern donors and Southern recipients. Previously an unquestioning attitude based on confidence and trust in individual ability, particularly in small-scale operations, has hindered the development of anything but personal evaluations which lack the soundness of more objective studies.

Specific cultural context of the project

Where traditional approaches to evaluation were not personal, they tended to take a short-term view, and the instrumental nature of such approaches meant that history and culture tended to get squeezed out, in the interests of developing standardised, objective measures. The re-oriented view of evaluation must recognise the context-specific nature of the project, as well as the essential subjectivity of the exercise — a tall order. Costs and benefits need to be calculated, but not necessarily in the ways that have been advocated for narrowly productive enterprises. The very nature of many social development projects and programmes makes it difficult, if not impossible, to make intelligent statements about efficiency, effectiveness, viability, and impact unless the specific cultural and socio-political environmental conditions of the particular place are given central attention.

This is not to say that things cannot be measured. Indeed the dichotomy between quantitative and qualitative data was seen during the conference as a false one, and something that inhibited rather than enhanced progress in thinking about evaluation. Numbers can become ends in themselves, rather than means to an end, and, as may be demonstrated in the contributions of participants to the conference, it is possible to put numbers on things which one might not have thought possible. The crucial issue is what importance is attached to the numbers, and knowing how they might be used and abused. While one might develop extensive arguments to dispute the methodologies associated with traditional evaluations, these should not be used to avoid evaluations *per se*. We

8

overestimate some of the problems that are associated with the use of quantitative data and techniques.

Questions of accountability

It is important, in this context, to be clear about the purpose of evaluation. At the moment the general consensus appears to be that it is too donor-led. Accountability should be shifted in line with the re-orientation of evaluation so that donors are themselves subject to some form of accountability. Traditional forms of evaluation based on short-term visits by outsiders, usually from the North, are helpful only in certain sorts of circumstances. A much wider basis for evaluation needs to be established. There needs to be much longer contact with beneficiary groups from which a more participative evaluation can be constructed and from which the groundwork for self-evaluation can be established. As a result of this longer time perspective, much richer material can be obtained and many gaps in the information base can be filled. In addition it provides the opportunity to be involved in the continuous process of monitoring and evaluation.

With this base it should then be possible to set clearer and more realistic objectives. The evaluation process itself should be seen as a way of providing space for the negotiation of objectives between donors and recipients which are much more likely to meet with success because they are based on more solid groundwork and an expanding trust which can encourage realism.

Context of evaluations

Let us not, however, divorce evaluation, and indeed the whole issue of social development, from the broader political and economic context in which it is embedded. We are concerned with the struggle of the poor and with the eradication of the causes of poverty. There is a danger that the whole social development project will be captured by regressive forces that will merely maintain the unequal *status quo* that currently prevails. Social development might then be seen as merely one element in a world-wide system which seeks to suppress genuine social and political grievances. Our concern to help grassroots movements involves a significant shift in the ways in which we approach development issues. The myth of the separation of the social from the economic, outlined in David Marsden's paper, allows us to marginalise social issues if we are not careful, so that they are seen as secondary to the seemingly more important economic concerns.

Many mistakenly assume that working for non-government organisations means working against the state. This is a naive simplification. While many of the policies which NGOs undertake might be oriented to the establishment, recovery, or defence of democracy, and as such be in opposition to those regimes which stand accused of inhibiting that development, it is necessary to work realistically through a thorough analysis of the particular socio-political environmental conditions that operate. The state is not some monolithic entity which is unchangeable. It represents a variety of interests and offers opportunities as well as constraints for change. The current climate presents particular challenges which need to be addressed. In many instances the retraction of the state from many areas of public provision provides exciting opportunities for NGOs to re-assess their relationships and their programmes. This is no easy task, and different organisations will approach it in different ways.

If we continue to see evaluations as primarily external impositions which aim to find fault and make judgements about shortcomings, then we make no progress. It should be recognised that grassroots groups are constantly evaluating what they do; they know that their work has value, they commit their time to it. It should also be recognised that they know that if they want external funding and external solidarity, then they will have to modify their accounting practices. But this modification should enhance performance, rather than encourage dependency. In order for this to occur, there will have to be a great improvement in the communication channels between donors and recipients.

It is recognised that reliable evidence of changes is required if funding is to be maintained. But therein lies an inherent paradox. If, from a re-negotiated evaluation, such reliable evidence is forthcoming, then, in the pursuit of self-reliance, this is a reason for discontinuing rather than maintaining funding. The problem of continuity of funds and the length of time necessary for support is a complex one.

The fundamental shift in the development of new evaluation methods comes from putting self-evaluation at the centre of the stage. This will not take place without a substantial transition. In the first instance there may be joint evaluations with both donors and recipients involved. This will evolve into the beneficiaries' evaluations of donor agencies, and ultimately to all involved in the project community putting their different interests on the table for public and open discussion.

The relationship between the project and development

Projects themselves are usually impositions on the community which includes the beneficiaries. The project itself does not constitute development. It is a mechanism which brings together different interests and pre-occupations to address particular issues and change particular circumstances. The separation of the project from the normal functioning of people's lives should be constantly borne in mind. Some would argue that a constantly evolving theme in the development process has been the attempt to create an even tighter fit between the realities of Southern communities and the imperatives of project aid. This is highlighted through a focus that has shifted from first-generation interventions which emphasised single issues (health care or agricultural extension, for example), through second-generation interventions that emphasised integrated development strategies, to third-generation interventions which emphasise smaller-scale, more qualitative and holistic development strategies which focus on hearts and minds in a much more intensive way and which try to penetrate the 'indigenous' institutions of society.

The danger with this 'progression' is that it is equally capable of generating instruments that can strengthen asymmetrical control as well as enhancing instruments for liberation. It can do the former by binding people more tightly into an international system over which the poor have very little control. It can do the latter by providing opportunities for the poor to develop strategies of resistance, and strategies to establish and maintain legitimate pressure groups in support of their 'rights'. Another potential danger with this more holistic focus is in the shift in emphasis from support for grassroots organisations to support for supposedly ailing, but established government institutions in the name of Institutional Development. This is echoed at the macro level in the demise of Integrated Area Development Programmes which attempted to by-pass existing institutional arrangements, but eventually succumbed to the attraction/ necessity/desirability of working through regular formal channels, rather than through separate boards or specially created organisations which gained their authority through attachment to the Prime Minister's or the President's office.

As we move to a more holistic approach, with all its inherent dangers and contradictions, it is important to focus not on the project, but on the organisation. The project remains merely the means whereby partnerships between organisations can be built and solidarity might be strengthened. Evaluation becomes a key tool in enabling this process. It provides an opportunity to articulate the different needs of both internal and external evaluations. The holistic approach is much more than a revamped integrated approach. The objectives of solidarity incorporate moral and spiritual dimensions which have rarely been addressed. One reason for this is the desire to pursue practical goals which have effects on productivity levels, but another reason must be the questioning of the North's moral and spiritual superiority following the historical experience of the colonial years. The colonial notion of the 'civilising mission' has been fundamentally contested, but apart from an awareness of cultural relativism and a respect for others, rooted in an egalitarian ethic, no other over-arching metaphilosophy has emerged.

The mutual relationship that is being recommended through attempts to construct solidarity must work towards the empowerment of people in the certain knowledge that they have secure support. But building alliances between different interest groups is no easy matter. It implies that members of different classes can build a common cause. The dangers of this developing into a paternalistic and hierarchical relationship are many. A re-negotiated evaluation process offers a way to confront and (ideally) overcome these dangers, by providing opportunities for the sensitive exploration of the values of different cultural systems, without the imposition of any one set of values. Through collective reflection on sub-stantive issues a negotiated consensus might be achieved, which effectively enhances the capabilities of all parties within the project community.

One feature that might disrupt this development is the rapid turnover of staff, especially in Northern NGOs. The process of shared evaluation is time-consuming and personal. Trust and solidarity are not easy things to legislate for, and are usually built through individuals. Translating this individual network into a set of institutional procedures is a key task in evaluation. The development of an institutional memory which transcends the individual experiences of transient workers is crucial to this task. A tour through the records of any NGO will reveal the partial nature of most project records which are not readily usable by people who do not know the projects.

Types and styles of evaluation

There are different types and styles of evaluation which are appropriate for different times and for different levels of interest within the project community. If evaluation is to become an educative and developmental tool, then the purposes of these different types and styles need to be clarified, and the levels and the times at which they might be most appropriately applied need to be identified.

Different people at different levels in the project community have different information requirements. One might identify at least three different levels — the level of the donor agency itself, the level of the intermediary managing institution, and the level of the beneficiaries. At all levels one might also identify three different types of information required. Firstly there is the need for a minimum of information on which to base decisions about project and programme funding and information on which to establish priorities. This might involve an analysis of social soundness, based on clear objectives and the establishment of base-line data, on which measurements of success can be founded. Secondly, there will be a wish to evaluate the legitimacy, authenticity and ability of the other actors in the project community. Thirdly, there will be a desire to evaluate the impact of the project — the efficiency and effectiveness by which funds were translated into action, and the impact on the lives of the beneficiaries.

To do all three might involve the use of a variety of techniques, ranging from the formal instrumental techniques associated with statistical manipulations, to evaluations that try to pick up less quantifiable understandings of progress through illuminative techniques, to evaluations, carried out by the beneficiaries themselves, which aim to review progress in their own terms and use such techniques as theatre, story telling, and communal meetings to achieve this.

Through the use of a suite of different techniques a more complete picture of process and progress can be built. Backward and forward linkages in communication channels can be established. Information is required by different members of the project community at different times. Through the successful combination and coordination of these different techniques, it should be possible to provide that information at appropriate times in order to respond to changing circumstances at all levels.

With the emphasis on building trust, partnership, and participation, the results of different evaluations should be made available to all parties and consolidated into a single text which is the basis of negotiations for the future. A re-negotiated evaluation strategy for the measurement of social development will mean that all techniques will be subordinated to the interests of securing solidarity.

Through this process the negotiation of the space for different value judgements will be facilitated. Behind such a negotiation are questions about the ownership and control of knowledge, and the uses to which it might be put. A sensitive handling of the process should ensure greater capacity to set objectives and define direction, to increase involvement of beneficiaries in operation and management, and to understand the implications (potentials and drawbacks) of using existing institutional channels. By attempting to dissolve the traditional distinctions which separate outsiders from insiders, a common goal might be pursued which allowed the representatives of Northern NGOs to develop a set of values that they were not afraid to espouse. As Esman and Uphoff maintain:

> We have to avoid the populist fallacy that ascribes only good intentions to the poor and malign intent to those in positions of power. (1984: 287)

Participatory self-evaluation depends on the notion of belonging. If the 'we' in the project community incorporates all levels, then self-evaluation must pervade all of those levels. Evaluation is then much more than providing useful information to decision makers; it is learning from people about their own methods of evaluation and incorporating that learning into a redesigned practice.

The text

The ensuing text is based largely upon the thematic papers presented to the conference, and on the outcomes of the group discussions — apart from Chapter 6, which ranges more broadly over the available literature in seeking to give a focus to future research in the area of the evaluation of social development. In all, six workshop papers are presented in the text in their original form; the rest of the book brings together summaries of other submitted papers, reports on the group discussions, and further bibliographical research.

A feature of Chapters 2-5 is the use of boxes in the text. Their purpose is two-fold. First, to introduce into the text material from other submitted papers, in order to give a flavour of the range of papers presented to the conference. Second, and most importantly, to illustrate an issue under discussion. The boxes serve as mini-case studies or examples of a particular aspect of the group discussions, and should be read in that light. They are not discussed in the text, but are located in such a way as to illustrate the immediate issue under discussion. The source of the material in the box is given, and readers could write to the author(s) directly if they wish to see the complete paper.

SECTION 1

THE MEANING AND EVALUATION OF SOCIAL DEVELOPMENT

1.1 The meaning of social development

David Marsden

Introduction

Thinking about social development is still couched within a national discourse about the provision of public facilities and the public bodies responsible for such provision. Such a national discourse is increasingly constricting and unrealistic, given the large numbers of multinational and transnational agencies concerned with the provision of development inputs, and the emergence of a 'global order'. National development strategies, the hallmarks of planning in the 1950s and 1960s, might now be considered to be part of the problem, rather than part of the solution. Attitudes to the formulation, implementation, and evaluation of development projects and programmes have also changed as the relevance of what has been termed 'sociological' knowledge has been reappraised and, indeed, has increased in significance (Cernea 1985 and Sutherland 1987), and as thinking about the most effective ways of distributing scarce public resources has changed.

Specific interests in social development date back to the 1950s, when the 'social' was separated from the 'economic' by the United Nations in their reports on the world social situation. The 'human factor' was seen to have been neglected in thinking about economic development, and sectoral analyses based on concerns with expanding social welfare provision were elaborated.

A new situation developed in the 1980s with the increasing recognition of the complexity of development intervention, and the need to understand social and political processes, to expand and enrich economic analyses, and to develop more appropriate tools in rapidly changing environments. Traditional frameworks appear to have exacerbated rather than reduced divisions between rich and poor, to have increased environmental instability, and to have made unrealistic or inappropriate demands on the political and social infrastructures available in many poor countries.

Social development planning has been consistently and fundamentally concerned with the eradication of poverty and the pursuit of equity in the identification of more holistic solutions to development problems. The concept of the 'unified' approach, outlined by the UN and adopted in the programmes elaborated by many of its agencies, forms a focus for this new thinking (Wolfe 1983). Far from being merely a question of technological fix and economic investment in industrial productivity, effective development can be accomplished only if the complex social structural issues which inhibit or channel development are themselves addressed.

Social development addresses problems of access to resources, the provision of basic needs, the distribution of those resources, the room to manoeuvre in straitened circumstances, and the effectiveness of the use of those scarce resources. It examines the different value premises on which policy decisions are made, and the contexts in which they are elaborated. It takes as its starting point the willingness of governments to intervene to direct development efforts, and to contribute resources to the satisfaction of basic needs and the redistribution of assets on a more egalitarian basis. But it also recognises the inability of many governments to intervene effectively, and the rising importance of what are termed non-governmental organisations (NGOs) in the provision of resources, to supplement those of governments.

A central issue is the exploration of more appropriate strategies for development which do not rely on outside resources, which encourage self-reliance and community participation, through more decentralised modes of decision-making. It cannot just be about the elaboration of specific social sectoral activities, but must aim to address wider issues in which such social sectoral concerns are rooted. It is only through an appreciation of the socio-cultural and political context in which development decisions are made that more appropriate managerial and decision-making tools can be developed.

Background

The background to the current debate is rooted in two approaches — the *sectoral* and the *holistic*. The sectoral approach separates out different spheres of activity for individual professional treatment. These spheres of activity (education, health, personal social services, and housing being the most notable) consume increasing proportions of the social product. The sectoral approach is based on a series of questionable premises. The first of these premises assumes that a distinction can be made between the 'public' and the 'private' domains, and that different criteria of performance should be used in their measurement and evaluation. A second premise assumes that particular aspects of human activity can be isolated for separate treatment, thus distinguishing between the different social sectors and those areas of responsibility which are governmental and those which are deemed not to be.

The sectoral (or specialist) approach and the more holistic (or generalist) approach have been complementary foci, and attempts to balance the two have been at the centre of interests in social development. Firstly there has been the traditional concern with social welfare activities, and the analysis of changes in the various social sectors and in thinking about the public provision of such facilities and resources (Hardiman and Midgley 1982). Secondly there is the more general concern with new directions in development policies as traditional strategies for intervention have been found wanting (McPherson 1982).

It is commonly believed that one of the major activities of government is to administer and supervise these 'public' domains. The debate within these sectoral domains is between the *residualists*, who maintain that government's role should be minimal, and the *substantivists*, who argue that more substantial government investment can serve a redistributivist role in the interests of greater equity and is a guarantee against exploitation and the exigencies of the free market. Behind all these discussions remains the question of social responsibility and the expected role of government in fulfilling its obligations. As is readily observable, there has been in the last few years a major debate about the limits to government, as questions of 'people power' are translated into issues of individual responsibility for the provision of what was formerly publicly provided, and as the legitimacy of governments and their ability to deliver and their legitimacy are seriously undermined.

The 'integrated' or 'holistic' approach, it might be argued, draws its inspiration from the tradition of political economy and is characterised by an understanding of the history of change, in which, in the field of interventions in the name of development, the planner, the policy maker, and the agents of change are seen as part of the analysis; in other words, it is recognised that they bring with them to the analysis their own biases, the results of their own, acknowledged, cultural heritage. In such an analysis it is recognised that 'sectoral' intervention of a narrow sort often fails to understand the interconnectedness of phenomena and is unlikely to achieve the desired aims. Because this approach operates 'above' the level of direct action, it is often perceived as being of less instrumental value.

The two approaches represent different movements in the social sciences (movements over time as well as in terms of theoretical underpinnings). They are rooted in different intellectual traditions. The first tends to be much more empirically based and instrumentalist, rooted as it is in the work of specific social sectors. It is concerned with getting a job done. The second approach is much more questioning and reflective. It is much more concerned with the analysis of the ways in which things are done. Traditionally the former approach has been associated with the 'positive practitioner' and the latter with the 'negative academic', and practice and theory have thereby been artificially divorced (Chambers 1983). The two approaches, however, are not necessarily to be perceived as mutually exclusive.

The 'sectoral' tradition has been very important in mapping out separate areas of expertise — health, social security, education, housing, personal social services — within what became known as the social services. It has built up major cadres of professionals who consume large amounts of public money and who generate their own justifications for maintenance and expansion. It is this apparently unending increase in the needs of such public services that has generated the debate about the limits to their growth, and has given rise to the search for alternative forms of provision as structural adjustments necessitate the re-alignment of government interests. This adjustment has been accompanied by attempts to rationalise service delivery and apply 'value for money' and more effective management criteria to public sector enterprises. If elements of these services can be devolved, then government expenditure can be reduced.

In the 1960s, social development meant the planning of the social services. As the welfare tradition within the UK and Western Europe developed, a comparative social policy also developed which used the same sectoral underpinnings. It was assumed that the major questions asked within Western Europe were also appropriate for the newly independent nations of the world and also that the world could be unquestioningly split into different sectors. The lessons that post-war Britain was learning were also applicable to her ex-colonies. Comparative social policy stressed continuity in provision, and took for granted the increasing responsibility of the state for social provision.

In the 1970s a more comprehensive understanding of the cultural differences which separated the European experience from that of the rest of the world developed as the naive faith in the efficacy of planning and the superiority of modern technology was questioned. There was a realisation that the models used to interpret social activity in Europe were often inappropriate to other contexts. There was a growing realisation that the administrative apparatus which had been developed in the North could not so easily be grafted on to the changing traditions of the South — cultural circumstances were different and resources were not available.

An anthropological relativism, with its roots in nineteenth century political economy, began to re-emerge as a knowledge of cultural differences and a questioning of different value systems became more widespread. The elaboration of different development paths stressed discontinuity rather than continuity, and a faith in unilinear development processes was replaced by an increased understanding of the complexity of the development task.

In addition, an alternative tradition, running counter to the received views about progress and development, gained a strong hold. This counter tradition incorporated an advocacy role for those working in the field of social development on behalf of the disadvantaged. It is suggested that the North and the rich were perhaps major causes of continued poverty in the world.

Social development has historically been associated with moral commitments to the excluded and the disadvantaged, and this has been a powerful force in moulding public opinion in favour of the legitimisation of activities aimed at alleviating poverty and attacking inequalities.

When this moral commitment, the execution of the work of socially responsible governments, is associated with a more holistic appreciation of such things as the distribution of political power and rewards, then the task of the social development worker has often appeared ambivalent: supporting the poor has often meant a challenge to the legitimacy of government action, as the worker explores those 'spaces' which might form the locus of opposition to forces which are deemed to be exploitative. Empowerment becomes a key concept.

Nevertheless the task was (and is) still informed by an analysis and a practice which stressed intervention in the name of responsible national governments and in the interests, and with the support of, their various publics. It was assumed that, despite cultural differences, the organisation of intervention could be systematised through the application of common administrative systems of management and organisation. The 'sectoral' approach was complemented by an ahistorical 'systems' approach.

In the 1980s times and ideas changed. International developments have created a very different environment in which development policies can be elaborated. The development of a global system requires the elaboration of different priorities. The myth of individual nations being able to act independently is frequently shattered by transnational institutions which operate in what are often termed subversive ways, undermining the authority and legitimacy of national governments. These institutions range from transnational companies through the multilateral aid agencies to organisations like the World Bank. They also include opposition forces of one kind or another, whether these are deemed legitimate or not, as well as the many NGOs working in various fields in the name of development.

There is a *crisis of legitimacy* which pre-empts the effective implementation of national development plans, by calling into question the role of government, and imposing limits on public spending. Legitimacy is threatened both internally and externally. The pendulum swings from concern for more effective and greater governmental control, to demands for government to get off the backs of the people. Public sector budgets show no signs of diminishing, and need to be checked. One solution is to devolve services to the 'private' and the 'voluntary' sectors. Another solution is to give local governments greater freedom to raise revenue and administer public services, with less support from the centre. The costs to central government can thus be reduced (although the costs to people may not be), and responsibility for failure devolved. Concerns for efficiency, economy, expediency, accountability, and cost-effectiveness echo the 'private' concerns of business. The international movement of funds to encourage development is contingent on governments removing 'unrealistic' subsidies on goods and services and decreasing public spending.

In a seemingly contradictory fashion the concerns to reduce the public burden by devolving responsibility for provision from the public sector to the private sector or from the centre to the provinces are upheld by those who support an integrated/holistic approach to development. The stress on appropriateness, on decentralisation, on self-reliance, on the participation of the public as 'active citizens', on sustainability, on building up local institutions, on getting rid of excessive and oppressive bureaucracies, on the use of para-professionals and volunteers, strengthens the attack on oppressive government and the dead hand of state intervention.

In all these areas at present there is intense ideological debate, as 'structural re-adjustment' is worked out in periods which are deemed by some to be characterised by extreme constraints on resources. The boundaries of state intervention are re-negotiated. The old orthodoxies are now in question. The radical alternatives built to challenge them are seemingly captured by the political forces which were formerly the bastions of tradition.

The changing focus

In such an international climate what should the foci of social development be? Should we maintain a sectoral focus — a focus which entrenches established interest groups? Or should we elaborate a more holistic approach, which implies a different way of seeing (what some have called a global perspective) as well as a different methodology for intervention?

Resource constraints, it might be argued, were felt in the Third World much earlier than in the developed world. Alternative forms of provision were already integral to many developmental approaches, as appropriate educational provision, primary health care, community care, and community-based approaches to the provision of social services were the norm rather than the exception. The more holistic approach to governmental intervention emerged of necessity in the search for effective development strategies, given very limited budgets and severe shortages of trained personnel.

Intervention seems to be characterised now by a preference for project-focused or issue-focused strategies which can combine the needs for more effective control over the disbursement of funds with the opportunities to work with more integrated packages in which the expenses associated with failures are limited in their impact. They provide opportunities to transcend existing bureaucratic structures. This is not only a characteristic of so-called Third World countries.

In such intervention the 'practical' appears to become divorced from the 'theoretical', but in actuality a very shallow theory which makes a virtue out of positivism and precludes an analysis of many otherwise controversial areas of social life is adopted. From the holistic perspective, theoretical analysis is inherent in any form of analysis, whether this is made explicit or not. Ahistorical model-building, involving the accumulation of 'lessons' from diverse case studies, tries to distil good practice and to generate 'practical' guidelines or manuals for successful replication. But because the analysis does not incorporate an historical understanding of the active role that Westerners play in shaping meaning, through their application of supposedly neutral scientific methods, this is little more than a classificatory exercise, based on the questionable premise that the more information one collects, the easier it is to see through the opaqueness of reality.

'Practical' considerations are popularly linked with economics — apparently the most practical of the social sciences used in development planning, and certainly the subject which has managed to generate the most legitimacy. By default this association tends to increase the connections that are made in the lay person's mind between the 'theoretical' considerations which are linked with the apparently least practical of the social sciences — sociology. The myth of separation between the social and the economic is thereby enhanced, and the inherent instability and marginality of social development planning seemingly guaranteed; the one is associated with generalism and the other with specialism. The one encompasses the residual areas which are not economic or economical (i.e. business-like) in their use of resources. A renegotiated focus must begin with a movement back to first principles, when the concerns that now characterise many of the social sciences were integrated into a more holistic political economy.

The separation of social development from applied social studies continued in the late 1970s as the anthropological relativism of strategies for intervention in the Third World dominated. It was deemed inappropriate to transpose European experiences on to Third World realities, on the assumption that this would encourage distorted and expensive public-sector investment, and discourage appropriate provision. The value premises on which Third World social policy should be elaborated were perceived as very different from those on which the European welfare state was based.

Paradoxically at the same time that the Third World was subject to such conceptual separation, various forces of change within European thinking ensured that such a distinction could not be easily maintained. The nature of multicultural societies in Europe, and the outlines of the 'World System' were becoming clearer. A new understanding, married to a recognition of the integrated nature of development strategies, and associated with an increasing realism, began to develop.

The demands for a type of understanding which recognised the different premises on which cultural values are based, which accompanied the expansion of cultural pluralism at home and abroad, fed into the evolving educational debate at all levels; development education was also about the development of education — the provision of more appropriate curricula with a more practical and a more comparative focus, informed by a new realism and greater public accountability. The involvement of patients, parents, and communities in health and educational provision served both to break the monopoly of established professions and to devolve responsibility.

The challenge

To ensure that real changes are forthcoming, attention must be focused on capacity building, through the development of more appropriate educational and organisational facilities. Attention must also be focused on the problems associated with the empowerment of the under-privileged. And if projects and programmes are to be more successful, the question of sustainability in an interdependent world must be addressed. This is not merely a question of environmental sustainability, but also of social and political sustainability.

The challenge which faces social development workers in the 1990s is one of responding to the changing world order. A radical redefinition of planning is required. As Sachs has suggested:

Planning must cease to be administrative and economistic and become visionary and pluridimensional ... Rather than claiming to be a set of techniques to orchestrate the efficient achievement of social objectives set by government, it should stress its eminently political goal as the organiser of the process of social apprenticeship by which men and women learn to identify their margins of freedom, invent the means by which they are put to profitable use and take the decisions which are essential for development. (Sachs 1987: 10-11)

In addressing this challenge, one might look at some of the implications this might have for those organisations concerned with teaching, training, consultancy, and research in the area of social development.

First, what is to be taught and who is to be taught? The question of appropriate training is a vexed one. Whose criteria for appropriateness are to be used? Is this to be left completely to the operation of the market, without any recognition of social responsibility — he who pays the piper calls the tune? Different methods of teaching need to be employed in order to stimulate critical awareness, and an understanding of alternative value systems and strategies and of competing interests and goals. The methodology employed operates from the local reality to develop a comparative and reflective understanding, which stresses the link between the local and the global. But a lack of standardisation means that performance is difficult to evaluate.

If the success of broad-based, integrated development projects is to be enhanced, then an approach which emphasises the cultural values and the modes of livelihood of the beneficiaries needs to be adopted. Time and time again the failure of projects is blamed on the inability to incorporate the 'human factor'. A balance must be achieved between the input of specialist knowledge and the need to reorient thinking. A greater understanding of the role of the practitioner in the process of development needs therefore to be emphasised; one which recognises that he or she is changed by as well as involved in changing reality, and one which recognises that he or she is part of the problem as well as part of the solution.

Who are to be trained, what are they to be trained in, and where are they to be trained? The aim of training is threefold: to provide workers with the appropriate tools, both conceptual and technical, to carry out their work more effectively; to make them aware of recent comparative developments within their fields of interest; to open up alternative ways of thinking and implementing social development programmes. Training thus combines sectoral with holistic approaches in attempts to provide access to and interpretations of current information, to cultivate a critical awareness of the issues involved in policy formulation and implementation, as well as to encourage the negotiation of realistic strategies based on a sound knowledge of local environments in which these policies will be implemented. Different methodologies for the incorporation of field practice need to be thought through.

New systems of accountability require re-orientation of academic and research effort. One of the major challenges from such a requirement to reorganise is presented by the need of sponsors to ensure 'value for money'. The requirements of private or public organisations imply the production of timely, appropriate, and usable reports. This is a challenge as well as a constraint. Here the academic establishment is in a strong position. Its position as a 'neutral' organisation with an in-built analytical capacity makes it potentially very useful for the provision of an external or objective analysis of policies, projects, and programmes. It is in a strong position to develop a 'social audit' function in the widest sense, in addition to the appraisal, monitoring and evaluation functions that it might also have.

We should not presume that any organisation has a monopoly over perceived wisdom, neither should we necessarily expect the findings of social science research to fit neatly into the boxes prescribed by development managers. One of the traditional roles of the social sciences has been to turn established explanations on their heads and come up with what might be rather uncomfortable results. This has been a major factor in the re-orientation of development thinking over the last 30 years.

We are not arguing necessarily for a separate professional category of 'social development worker', but rather for the recognition of a re-oriented attitude to interventions in the name of development. In a way it is the qualitative and intuitive strengths of the social analyst which are at a premium. As norms of accountability change, the distinctions between abstraction and manipulation, between pure and applied research, also change.

The current focus on local-level, participatory development strategies encourages a move to qualitative and intuitive analyses (in the absence of more formal quantitative models, and given the partial views of reality that are obtainable). But the aim should not necessarily be to 'domesticate' these intuitive analyses into prescriptive formulas incorporated into a more complex model with predictive power, but rather to use them to engage in the creation of alternative developmental paths in which development projects are seen as policy experiments and subject to constant re-adjustment (Rondinelli 1983).

We are often presented with the unsubstantiated statement that sociology and social anthropology have not yet matured, and that all that is needed for their more effective incorporation in the establishment of development practitioners is more sophisticated theory and an opportunity to 'catch up' with the more 'advanced' disciplines, notably economics, which are at the centre of development intervention. This also needs to be questioned. It is based on the assumption that more effective intervention is somehow interlinked with the ability to construct and manipulate more sophisticated models. In reality, effective intervention strategies appear much more dependent on the right people being in the right place at the right time, and no amount of planning or model building can assure that.

What is needed is courage. Courage on the part of managers of development projects and programmes to entertain and indeed encourage the innovative and the speculative, and courage on the part of social scientists to resist incorporation into an 'industry' over which they have little control. There is still a place for intellectual freedom, room to manoeuvre and for theoretical contributions which transcend narrow pre-occupations. The art is to be able to 'speak truth to power' (Wildavsky 1979), which is perhaps one of the reasons why so much attention is currently devoted to development discourse associated with the representation of that truth, and its use in the transformation of an increasingly literate society. While he who pays the piper may call a tune, that tune is of another's invention and its particular rendition is in response to particular circumstances.

1.2 The evaluation of social development

Peter Oakley

If some form of social development is to become the objective of a particular development programme or project, then it is reasonable to assume that, at some stage in the project's evolution, we may wish to evaluate its outcome or impact. As we have seen in the previous paper, however, we are dealing with interpretations of social development which lack the tangible parameters of social development as the provision of social services, and which confront us with a form of development which is also intangible and less amenable to quantitative measurement. Since interpretations of social development began to move into these less tangible areas in the mid-1970s, we have encountered problems of understanding and explanation. More specifically we have encountered problems related to the evaluation of such projects. Remarkably, and despite the fact that there is widespread support for this form of social development project — particularly among the NGOs — little progress has been made in developing the means to understand better both the functioning and effect of these projects. Social development projects are now a recognisable feature of development activity, and yet their evaluation is either overlooked or at best done in a limited fashion. This conference is a forum for beginning to begin to tackle this dilemma.

The dominant evaluation paradigm

The concept of evaluation is a clearly recognised and understood aspect of development programmes and projects. There is a vast corpus of literature of both a conceptual and an applied nature which supports evaluation activities. Projects are the basic instruments of development intervention, and evaluation is crucial to understanding the results of these interventions. Evaluation is to do with measurement, judgement, and analysis, and is critical in terms of ensuring that any project is moving towards and accomplishing its intended objectives. Evaluation activities should be relevant, timely, and accurate and should produce the information and data required to understand the progress of a project. Ideally evaluation should be built into a project's organisational and implementation structure, and should be undertaken as a continuous and systematic activity during the lifetime of a project. Arguments for evaluation stress the importance of providing project staff with the information needed to assess a project's progress, in terms of its objects, and to make any corresponding mid-term adjustments; equally they point to the need to justify expenditure and to estimate the returns to a particular level of investment. Evaluation has become the exercise whereby an assessment can be undertaken of the impact of a project, and decisions made concerning replication, extension, or the closing down of project activities.

As project interventions are broadly dominated by a perspective which sees development largely in tangible, physical terms, so the practice of evaluation is dominated by an approach which reflects this development perspective. This dominant interpretation of evaluation is concerned with *measurement*, with giving a numerical value to the supposed outcome of a development project. It is concerned with the *effort* expended, the *effect* of the project in terms of its original objectives, and the *efficiency* of the project in terms of the use of resources. Essentially this approach to evaluation measures a project's tangible or material performance, and overwhelmingly this performance tends to be the sole criterion for judgement on the project's outcome. The most widely used analytical tool of this form of evaluation is *cost-benefit analysis (CBA)*, which is a quantitative formula for assessing the merits of a project in terms of the returns to investment. This approach to evaluation is entirely relevant to the tangible or material outcomes of a project, and should present an acceptable quantitative understanding of project success or failure.

Despite its widespread use and acceptance, this dominant paradigm of evaluation is not without its critics. One area of criticism is more technical in nature and revolves around the twin issues of attribution and causality. In other words, when evaluating in strictly quantitative terms, what is the cause-effect link between the project and the ostensible outcome; and secondly, how far can perceived outcomes be attributed to project activities? Furthermore, within a paradigm that accepts in principle the need for cost-benefit analysis, there are criticisms of a technical nature relating to CBA costs, procedures, and potential for manipulation. More substantially, however, criticism of this dominant paradigm suggests that it is essentially a limited and static form of evaluation which is unable to reflect adequately the outcomes of projects which are not exclusively quantitative in nature. It is also time-consuming: its techniques can often lead to major evaluation exercises which absorb the time and energies of project staff. Furthermore, it is suggested that this approach has a built-in bias towards favourable quantitative outcomes, and rarely reflects the unforeseen consequences of project interventions. Essentially it is argued that this evaluation paradigm is externally conceived and implemented, it takes little note of the people who directly experience the realities of the project's outcome, it is limited in its vision to what can be quantified and measured, and it is totally unable to encompass or explain non-material or non-tangible development objectives. In other words, although it is acceptable as a way of understanding one particular form of project outcome — that which is tangible and quantitative — it is inadequate as a basic technique to evaluate social development.

The evaluation of social development

Since the early 1960s there has been an increasing tendency to evaluate social development programmes and projects. This practice was largely influenced by North American scholars and drew extensively upon the above evaluation paradigm for its model. Social development in this practice was understood more in a social welfare or social service sense, and was seen as the social dimension to the more dominant, economic basis of development. Social development meant education, health services, and welfare provision, and was evaluated largely in quantitative terms. Social cost-benefit analysis emerged as an accompanying technique to evaluate these social programmes. More broadly concepts such as the *social effects* of projects, the *social impact* of projects or *social indicators* have all emerged in the past twenty years or so as indications of an increasing wish to get beyond the purely economic and into the social outcomes of development projects. Yet these approaches still fall broadly within the dominant evaluation paradigm, in that they seek to measure and to give a numerical value to the social outcomes of development. While this is entirely valid and acceptable, it is limiting in terms of our understanding of social development. While the above are useful supports, they are less helpful in evaluating the non-material dimension of social development and the *process* nature of social development activities.

To begin to understand the issues involved, we can refer back to Marsden's paper on social development, and indeed the interpretation of social development as presented in the background information to this conference. While not suggesting that social development is an entirely qualitative process, nor wishing to argue that the above approaches to the evaluation of social development are totally irrelevant, we do need to recognise that in this conference we shall be concerned with the evaluation of a particular interpretation of social development. This interpretation is not easy to encompass within a single definition; more importantly it is not possible to understand it in purely quantitative terms. This difficulty is reflected in the kinds of objectives associated with this interpretation of social development. The following are some examples of the objectives of the type of social development project which we shall be examining:

Help women to develop their awareness of the conditions that dominate their lives and of their subordinate role; and thus promote their organisation and participation in the process of social change. (War on Want, Peru 5)

The main objective of the project is to help the rural masses to educate themselves, so that they will be able to critically assess their situation, organise themselves as a powerful group, and creatively work to change society towards building up a new world. It is a programme of adult education in order to dispel wrong attitudes, create new ones, and awaken people to revolutionise social structures so that they can be the masters of their own destiny. (CAFORD, Sri Lanka 59)

The programme of women's meetings is being organised to fulfil its main objective of helping women who are suppressed to raise their voices. We are starting our programme with women's literacy, and will work towards awareness-building and consciousness-raising among the villagers through their organisations. (Oxfam, India/UDP 0811)

a. Fight local conformist feelings and help develop a more participatory outlook.
b. Develop local knowledge and encourage peasants to use their knowledge as the basis for understanding the issues which confront them.
c. Develop leadership within the people.
d. Encourage the peasants to take over the organisation themselves. (Christian Aid, Brazil 13a)

a. To promote adequate forms of self-help groupings and organisation of subsistence farmers, which they regard as their own, for the satisfaction of their specific economic and social needs.
b. To identify, plan and implement income-generating activities for and with such groupings with a view to increasing economically viable group action.
c. To increase the effectiveness of the service delivery system and to stimulate improved access for the rural excluded to existing programmes and services. (FAO/PPP)

The central issue of the conference, therefore, is how we could evaluate these kinds of objectives; assuming, of course, that the concept of evaluation is the appropriate term. Let us for the moment assume that it is, and also that there is a genuine interest in approaches and methods which might help us to evaluate without bias the outcome of objectives such as the above.

In the first instance it must be said that at this moment we are not in a very strong position to evaluate objectives such as those above. The search began over ten years ago to construct an approach to evaluation which might be more relevant to the interpretation of social development as presented in this conference. This search has not been entirely successful, and this has been a major reason for the organisation of this event. In comparison with the vast corpus of theoretical literature and practical material which support the evaluation of quantitative development projects, there is a paucity of support for the evaluation of social development projects.

The issue, therefore, is how to understand and evaluate such non-material and non-directly production-related objectives of social development projects. Conventional evaluation is dominated by a concern to measure; but how can we 'measure' qualitative change? Imboden (1980) highlighted this dilemma when she suggested that there were certain dimensions of development projects which were not amenable to measurement in quantifiable terms. Concepts of social development such as, for example, *participation* are difficult to define solely in specific, quantifiable terms. Unlike, for example, a credit programme to finance the purchase of fertiliser, which we can judge in terms of the take-up of credit, the magnitude of fertiliser application, or the eventual level of crop production, a process of participation might not follow such a predictable path. Social development objectives are not only difficult to characterise, but it is also difficult at the beginning of a project to predict what their outcome or effect might be. Beforehand, it will be difficult to spell out precisely how objectives such as 'participation' might manifest themselves, and what their eventual nature might be.

We need an approach to evaluation, therefore, which is not based exclusively on the measurement of material outcomes, but which is able also to explain what happens in a social development project which seeks to promote the kinds of objectives we have seen. Participation, for example, like poverty, is an abstract concept and, although we can attribute material or productive characteristics to the process involved, such characteristics are inadequate as the only means of explaining its many potential dimensions. In other words, in dealing with non-material objectives of social development, we are concerned not only with *results* which are *quantitative*, but more importantly with *processes* which are *qualitative*. These objectives are phenomena which occur over time, and they cannot be measured simply by a single 'snap-shot' form of exercise. They are processes which unfold throughout the life of a project, and ideally continue when the project formally ceases, and they have a range of characteristics and properties. The evaluation of social development objectives, therefore, will involve a number of quantifiable aspects; it will also involve a less predictable number of qualitative aspects.

Qualitative evaluation is more concerned with *describing* the characteristics and properties of a process like participation, for example, over a period of time, and then with *interpreting* the data and information available in order to make statements concerning the nature and extent of the participation which has occurred. The nature of qualitative evaluation, therefore, is different from that of quantitative evaluation, and it demands different indicators, different methods of collection, and different analysis. It has implications for the practice of evaluation in social development projects and suggests the need to broaden and re-think the basis of this practice.

Before we examine specific approaches to the evaluation of social development, we could suggest a number of key principles which should guide this evaluation. These principles are based upon a review of the (albeit limited) practice to date, but collectively they provide a basis for the implementation of this type of evaluation.

1 The evaluation of social development projects is *qualitative* as well as *quantitative*: both dimensions of social development must be included for a full understanding of the outcome.

2 It is *dynamic* as opposed to *static*: the evaluation of social development demands that the entire process over a period of time be evaluated, and this requires more than a limited snap-shot. Conventional retrospective evaluation, therefore, will not be adequate.

3 *Monitoring* is of central importance: the evaluation of a process of social development is impossible without relevant and continual monitoring. Indeed, monitoring is the key to the whole exercise, and the only means by which the qualitative descriptions can be obtained to explain the process which has occurred.

4 Evaluation must be *participative*: in the entire evaluation process, the people involved in the project have a part to play. It is not a question of an external evaluator solely determining the project outcome; the local people themselves will also have a voice.

Approaches to qualitative evaluation

While the practice will encompass supporting tangible and material activities, social development is essentially a *process*, and it is this process which we wish to evaluate. While not wishing to question the importance of such material activities to social development, our concern in this conference is to find ways to improve the evaluation of the more qualitative aspects of social development. The process of social development is qualitative and presents both conceptual and practical problems in its evaluation. In terms of social development as interpreted at this conference, the issue of its qualitative evaluation is still in its infancy. The concept of qualitative evaluation owes much of its development to North American scholars; Weiss (1972), Merton et al. (1979), Cook and Reichardt (1979), and Patton (1987), for example, have contributed to developing an understanding of this particular dimension of evaluation, although it must be noted that they have written exclusively in a North American context. The works of Parlett and Hamilton (1972), Patton (1987) and Richards (1985) are particularly important in suggesting the critical dimensions of qualitative evaluation. Richards' study of a Cultural Action Programme in Chile is perhaps the only detailed account to date of the practice of the qualitative evaluation of a social development programme. Reviewing the conceptualisation of qualitative evaluation in these studies (or *Illuminative Evaluation*, as Parlett and Hamilton call it), we can note a number of key themes which may help to give some shape to the central issue of this conference:

1   Qualitative evaluation is *naturalistic*, in the sense that the evaluator does not attempt to manipulate the programme or its participants for the purposes of the evaluation. Naturalistic enquiry studies processes as they occur, and not on the basis of a pre-planned experiment. As a social development process unfolds, a naturalistic approach would be sensitive to changes in direction, unexpected outcomes and differential impact. Since naturalistic enquiry is not locked into searching only for pre-determined and expected outcomes, it is able to identify and describe what actually happens as a result of a project.

2   Qualitative evaluation similarly is <u>heuristic</u>, in that the evaluation approach is subject to <u>continuous redefinition</u> as our knowledge of the project and its outcomes increases. Qualitative evaluation does not restrict itself to pre-formulated questions or lines of enquiry; rather it evolves, by observable changes being followed up and new questions coming to the fore. The evaluation starts with intensive familiarisation and develops the

33

exercise as a series of stages, thus building up a comprehensive understanding of the activities being evaluated.

3 Qualitative evaluation is *holistic*, in that the evaluation exercise sees the programme as a working whole which needs to be both understood and analysed from many different perspectives. This holistic approach ensures that detailed attention is given to the different dimensions of a social development project: context, participants, interrelationships with other projects, activities, and so on.

4 Qualitative evaluation employs *inductive analysis*, in the sense that the evaluator seeks to understand the outcome of a social development project without imposing pre-determined expectations. This inductive approach begins with specific observations and builds towards general patterns of project outcome; the evaluator gathers qualitative data on programme outcome through direct observation of programme activities and in-depth interviews with participants, without being limited to stated, pre-determined evaluation goals. The approach is also essentially *interpretative*, built up through description of the significant facts, figures, and characteristics of the project which are an accurate reflection of its overall complexity. This continuous interpretation provides the raw material which forms the basis of the project's evaluation.

5 Qualitative evaluation, by its very nature, implies a *continuous and close contact with the participants of a programme* in their own environment. The qualitative approach emphasises the importance of getting close to project participants in order to understand more authentically their realities and the details of their everyday lives. The evaluator intensifies this close contact through physical proximity for an extended period of time as well as developing a closeness resulting from the shared evaluation experience. Qualitative evaluation demands participation and commitment of the evaluator and discourages detachment and distance, which are characteristics of other approaches to evaluation.

Qualitative evaluation sees social development projects as *dynamic* and *evolving* and not necessarily following a pre-determined direction. The approach, therefore, can be responsive to innovative projects and, more importantly, to objectives which are not easily measurable. The approach of qualitative evaluation draws considerably upon the *phenomenology* school of social enquiry. Emphasis is put upon the identification of key phenomena within any given context, and on the systematic recording and interpretation of activities and changes around these phenomena. Qualitative evaluation also re-defines the nature and activities of the *evaluator*, by linking the evaluator both ideologically and physically with project activities, and by stressing that evaluation studies should inform, add to understanding, and be responsive and readable and not merely destined for academic journals.

Issues for consideration

1 The qualitative evaluation of processes like social development poses an immediate important question: *how far are conventional cost-benefit and cost-effectiveness analyses relevant to this form of evaluation?* In one sense qualitative evaluation poses the issue of how far we should be influenced by these formulas of conventional evaluation. Richards' (1985) study on Cultural Action in Chile, in which project practitioners saw little relevance in the cost-effectiveness approach for evaluating their work, is particularly pertinent in this respect. Perhaps for the moment we are unable to answer the above questions, but we should bear in mind the need to examine these conventional tools of analysis in the light of social development projects. Few studies exist to guide us in this matter, yet they remain pertinent questions to pose.

2 *The qualitative evaluation of social development almost certainly demands its own particular methodology.* Qualitative evaluation will be based upon key criteria or indicators which will illustrate the processes unfolding; this will involve methods of data and information collection pertinent to the exercise; it will also imply the interpretation of the data and information in a manner which will help us judge the outcomes of the project.

3 Similarly the qualitative evaluation of social development probably implies *a different evaluation design.* We have seen the basis of this design in earlier parts of this paper. Essentially, as Patton (1987) remarks, we are moving 'beyond the numbers game' and as such into a very different form of evaluation. Richards (1985), for example, sees the move away from what he calls 'preordinate objectives' as fundamental to this new approach, with the emphasis in evaluation design upon responsiveness, and suiting the evaluation design to the unfolding situation and not rigidly to already identified objectives. Evaluation design also refers to structure, format, methods of data storage and also of results publication.

4 The *timing* of an evaluation is also an issue for examination. Conventionally and almost always project evaluation occurs either mid-term or on the completion of a recognised phase of project activities. In many of the latter instances such evaluation becomes an attempt to understand what has taken place, often based on limited or sporadic data and information. Qualitative evaluation, on the other hand, by its very nature implies some kind of continuous exercise of data collection and interpretation.

Qualitative evaluation has emerged in the past two decades as a means to broaden the repertoire of evaluation tools available to practitioners. For too long the evaluation of development programmes and projects has mostly conformed to one dominant model; but there may now be a consensus that it is important to match the situation with the appropriate evaluation tools. Qualitative evaluation still faces challenges on the issue of *objectivity* and the supposed subjective nature of its methodology; but its legitimacy is being more widely accepted and its relevance to the evaluation of social development increasingly recognised.

Concluding comments

This paper has not presented a model for the evaluation of social development programmes and projects. Even if such a model existed, it would be difficult to argue that it was universally applicable. The purpose has been to present the issue conceptually and also to present a broad framework of issues which we can use in considering other material presented in the conference. This framework inevitably gives rise to the core material in the evaluation of social development: methodology, indicators, partnership and the role of the evaluator — and these will each be taken up in subsequent papers. An important issue before us here is that, although this paper has presented a conceptual framework for the qualitative evaluation of social development, it has drawn largely on literature from a context entirely different from the Third World, and it has found few practical studies of relevance. It should be seen as a guide to our discussions and analysis in the conference with the view to formulating a statement more relevant to social development in the Third World. Our concern in this conference is to see if we can begin to construct an appropriate framework for the evaluation of social development (if 'evaluation' is indeed the appropriate word), and identify and characterise methodologies and procedures which might support this framework.

Our discussions should take place against the background of several broader issues related to the evaluation of social development. Evaluation is not a neutral or ideologically untainted activity, and it does not take place in a vacuum. While we must concern ourselves in the workshops with developing a practical framework for evaluation, this must be done with these broader issues in mind:

1 Does the evaluation of social development imply a fundamental questioning of the nature of evaluation? Evaluation is more commonly seen as a structured activity, usually externally initiated, with a paraphernalia of evaluation designs, questionnaires, and data-processing techniques. Does the evaluation of social development even question the use of the term 'evaluation', and do we need to consider an alternative terminology? In short, *does the evaluation of a process like social development demand a different action, with a different vocabulary and different instruments?*

2 Whatever its nature, evaluation is not a value-free exercise. Conventional evaluation approaches are often criticised for the implicit value assumptions they make in judging programme or project performance. The very term 'evaluation', with its implicit suggestion of 'judgement', is value-laden, and it would appear impossible to construct an 'evaluation' exercise which is neutral. *Will indeed it be possible to construct a framework for the evaluation of social development which is value-free?* If not, how can we build this inherent bias into our framework at least to mitigate its impact?

3 Inevitably in evaluation exercises, some people take the lead, give direction, and carry out the evaluation on the assumption that the results of the exercise will authentically represent both the project outcome and the views of those who experienced the project's activities. In evaluating social development, *how can we safeguard the authenticity of the exercise, so that we can be unreservedly sure that its outcome is a faithful reflection of the actual situation?* What pre-conditions need we establish to ensure this authenticity, and how and by whom would these pre-conditions be agreed? Primarily in the evaluation of social development we must strive to avoid the accusation that the picture presented is an external construct and not a true reflection of reality.

4 The evaluation of social development may well cause us to question exactly what it is that we are seeking to evaluate? Evaluation exercises are invariably dominated by objectives — normally preordinate objectives which the evaluator uses to measure outcome — as opposed to being equally concerned with outcomes within the broader project context. When we evaluate social development, therefore, *should we take a holistic view and seek to understand project outcome more generally, or merely limit the exercise to the preordinate objectives?*

5 Does the evaluation of social development imply an emphasis upon an examination of practice to help construct the theoretical basis of the evaluation, or *must established theory always determine the nature of the evaluation?* Should we think of turning things around and starting off with the practice, or do we always need the security of this established theory before we undertake an evaluation?

The purpose of this conference, therefore, is to structure, describe, and detail an appropriate approach, framework and methodology for the evaluation of social development. It will not be an easy task. In his impressive study on the Evaluation of Cultural Action, Richards (1985) faced the same challenge and concluded that

> ... no minor tinkering will suddenly bring the usually taught and practiced methods of evaluation up to scratch; it is not a case of this powerful school of social science research having a few easily corrected flaws, some practical limitations requiring a little adjustment here and there to make it fit evaluation's demands. No, what is needed for a truly sensible evaluation methodology is an entire shift of perspective in fundamental assumptions, working concepts, methodological tenets and research values. When this total re-think of evaluation occurs, the almost slavish-seeming adherence to dominating conventions of formal research design, elaborate statistical procedures, etc., is inevitably broken, as strategies, goals and outcomes become redefined to accord more with the realities of everyday phenomena and less with methodological dictates.

Whether this conference can in the space of two and a half days bring about an 'entire shift of perspective' in the evaluation of social development is debatable, but at least we can give it a try!

SECTION 2

QUALITATIVE DIMENSIONS OF SOCIAL DEVELOPMENT EVALUATION

2.1 Qualitative dimensions of social development evaluation: Thematic paper

Muhammad Anisur Rahman

Today for the first time the tribal labourers of this area are going on strike, stopping work on their own initiative. This may result in a wage rise of say Rs 100 per year or RS 50 per year — What is important to us, however, is that we are asserting that we too are human beings.

(Ambarsingh Suruwanti, a tribal labour leader in Maharastra, India, 1 May 1972)

Introduction

Although the subject of this conference concerns 'projects and programmes in the Third World', this paper offers thoughts towards an overall orientation on the question of qualitative dimensions of social development, at the grass roots as well as at higher levels. It is argued that, keeping in view the considerations presented in this paper, actual indicators for evaluating social development in any specific project or programme must be developed in the concrete context of the project or programme's specific objectives, its socio-economic context and the people's culture. Furthermore any evaluation will be developed by the project community, i.e. the people concerned and others who will have a responsibility for implementation. Project and programme evaluation is considered also to be a learning process for the project community, and indicators should be subject to progressive refinement or modification as experience is gained and ideas develop. Finally, there is no reason why the concern for social development and its evaluation should be restricted to the Third World.

For the sake of convenience, social science and development cooperation have had an overwhelming bias towards quantitative indicators for assessing developmental progress. This has been unfortunate and has generally given a distorted approach to development policy and action.

Imagine the development of a human child to be assessed in terms only of indices such as his or her physical health, grades in school, and eventually his or her financial earnings. A 'well-developed' person in such terms may very well be a social nuisance and/or a very miserable person, even in a reasonably normal social environment. It is perfectly natural and valid to want to see one's child develop as a wholesome human personality, making a comfortable but not necessarily lavish living, able to handle life's tensions without cracking, developing creative faculties of social value, emotionally content with life, loved by family and friends, and held in broad respect by the wider society. Most such indicators of personal development are not quantitatively measurable, but they may nevertheless be at the core of enlightened human aspirations, for oneself as well as for one's children. There is no reason why, for society or communities of people, the notion of development should be very different, and should take a narrower, predominantly quantitative, view, leaving out vital considerations which can be assessed by analytical reasoning if they cannot be measured by numbers.

Popular needs and priorities: some examples

One may ask whether for materially poor communities the question of access to the so-called 'basic needs', i.e. food, clothing, shelter, education and health care, are not of overriding importance so as to constitute the core indicators of progress which are quantifiable anyway. I have often sought to test this question myself, on various occasions, in dialogues with poverty groups who have become mobilised for collective struggle and endeavours to improve their lives. Some have, indeed, indicated a bias predominantly oriented towards 'basic needs' in expressing their aspirations, although it has often appeared that they are repeating what they are being told by some quarters. I have also heard people say that they did not know that they were 'poor', before they were told so. But there have been others who have responded differently.

For example, in a dialogue with leaders and cadres of the Bhoomi Sena movement in Maharastra, India (de Silva et al., 1977), there arose the question of why bonded labour was selected as the first issue to be tackled. The reply was, 'It was a question of human dignity. The reason was not economic only.' One could argue that the question of bonded labour itself, in any case, could be handled quantitatively. But human dignity is affronted in many other ways, with various modes of personal and social humiliation including physical humiliation, sexual abuse, and outright assault, backed by the social status and the power of the offenders.

There are numerous organised groups of disadvantaged people around the world who are struggling not only for economic rights, but also for human rights. I had a most revealing experience in Bangladesh, when an assembly of organised landless rural workers' groups who had been struggling for economic and other rights for about eight years without any significant gain in their economic status asserted that their lives nevertheless had changed, and that they would never give up their organisation because 'the elites have to talk to us with respect now that we are organised' (Rahman 1986). In times of flood-stricken distress other groups have expressed a similar comment: 'If they cannot give us wheat, OK, but we shall not accept the abuses. They must treat us as human beings...' (Rahman 1987). Furthermore, groups of very poor rural women who became organised stated that one of the greatest gains to them from organising had been the opportunity and ability they gained just to talk in public, and as a result they tried to attend every meeting to share their problems and seek solutions. This they did both to gain some freedom and to experience a sense of solidarity with other women, in an environment where customarily they stayed in and around their immediate families and did not have the right to speak in the presence of an adult male, except close relations. For this experience alone they considered that the development of their organisation had constituted a profound change in their life (Rahman 1987).

More poignant was the rejection of an elitist notion of 'development' by a number of forest-based poor people's movements in India, after a process of joint reflection on their status:

... We have seen and we have tried to present the picture of degradation of our culture ... The life of a forest-dweller has many compensations which are not available to city dwellers ... For 'development' we have to give up our life style and our culture and ... we are gradually imbibing the culture and life of the slums ... We feel cheated ... It is strange that what is good for us has been decided by those who have cheated us and the country. They have deprived us of our habitat and the country of her environment ... Those who are interested in a new forest policy are not the forest-dwellers. Their major interest is the development of forest as a resource, rather than as a habitat of the people. This basic difference distinguished 'us' from 'them'. They believe that we (the forest dwellers) should reap the dubious benefits of 'development'. Or, in other words, become like them or their serfs. We have tried in this report to show how we have lived for centuries — sheltered, protected and nurtured by the forest.

This lifestyle is now fast disappearing along with the forest ...
(Dasgupta 1986, chapter 6)

A different dimension of people's self-assessment of progress was revealed in an evaluation of a project in the Philippines which provided animation work to promote organisations of various categories of rural workers in four villages (Rahman 1983). The organisations were engaged in collective activities which brought economic gains in different degrees to their members. A random sample of the members of these organisations were interviewed, and people were asked what was the most important benefit they had gained by organising. Without exception, every one of them replied 'education'; the gaining of knowledge, through actual experience, that they could improve their status by organising and working together, was the single most important benefit they had gained. No one, even out of those whose economic status had improved substantially, mentioned economic gain as the most important.

More such examples could be given of people's perceptions of 'progress' or 'development'; perceptions and priorities in terms of dimensions of life which are not readily quantifiable and are yet of profound value to the people. But let us end this section by recalling the following revealing observation in a discussion of the ORAP movement (Organisation of Rural Associations for Progress) in Matabeleland, Zimbabwe:

Significantly, the translation of the concept of development into Sindebele (local language of Matabeleland) is 'taking control over what you need to work with'. The names of most ORAP groups also reflect these concerns. A few chosen at random are: Siwasivuka (We fall and stand up), Siyaphambili (We go forward), Dingimpilo (Search for life), Sivamerzela (We're doing it ourselves), Vusanani (Support each other to get up) ... (Chavunduka et al., 1985)

As I have observed elsewhere (Rahman 1989), in apparently naive words these expressions of people's collective self-identity reflect deep conceptualisations of popular aspirations. Hence they reflect implicit popular notions of 'development'. The people want to stand up, take control over what they need to work with, to do things themselves in their own search for life, to move forward, supporting each other. These are as much part of their 'basic' needs as the 'basic needs' of conventional development thinking. These are holistic needs, or aspirations, which cannot be quantified without distorting their basic spirit.

Finally, when I recently visited a relatively well-off village in Hungary, members of the community claimed that efforts to promote participatory development are no less needed for the 'rich', and that 'what hurt most is the indignity of being forced to vote for a chairman who I know is corrupt'. This indignity is a measure of one's poverty, notwithstanding one's material well-being, and a measure, therefore, of social underdevelopment.

Who assesses development?

So far this discussion has suggested that there are certain qualitative dimensions of life to which ordinary, disadvantaged or underprivileged people — whether materially poor or rich — attach considerable importance, given their specific situations and conditions of life. The basic moral of the examples quoted above is that such people have their own views about what they value in life. Their views may or may not coincide with ours, rooted as we are in a very different life with a very different evolution which has shaped our perceptions about what is valuable. In this context, when we talk about indicators of social development, quantitative or qualitative, a basic question that has to be faced concerns the legitimacy of ourselves, intellectuals and social development practitioners or promoters, sitting in judgement over what constitutes social development or not. Furthermore, how far can we go in articulating what should essentially be the prerogative of the people themselves to articulate?

There is no escape from these questions. Our legitimacy in these matters may perhaps be rationalised in terms of the social power we possess, and have chosen to exercise, to try to influence the process of social development of some societies in a more participatory direction, about whose dimensions we have some visions both of our own as well as derived from our interaction with people at the grass roots. However, given that the thinking of the people themselves may not necessarily coincide with ours, the absence of an authentic people's point of view remains a serious limitation on how confidently we can determine the dimensions of social development. At best, our views must be considered tentative, subject to validation or modification by the local community. In fact, a process of *empowering and enabling* the people to articulate and assert, by words and by deeds, their ideas and thinking in this regard, must be one of the core dimensions of social development itself. Social development cannot begin if the people are unable to express and assert what social development means to them. This, then, is a fundamental indicator of social development in societies where such empowerment still remains a distant dream and, unfortunately, it could be argued that this is the prevalent state of affairs in many nation states today.

Elements of empowerment

A quantitative element of empowerment is control over economic resources; but progress in this matter is by itself no indication of enhanced social power of the underprivileged to assert their developmental aspirations and their freedom to take initiatives for their self-development. The essential qualitative elements of empowerment are well suggested in many writings on participatory development, from which I would highlight three:

1 *Organisation* of the disadvantaged and underprivileged people in structures under their own control, of sufficient strength, derived from direct numerical size and/or linking with other organisations of similarly situated people.

2 *Social awareness* of the disadvantaged, in terms of understanding derived from collective self-enquiry and reflection, of the social environment of their lives and the working of its processes. The knowledge itself, and a feeling of knowing from self-enquiry, are both important in giving the disadvantaged a sense of equality with the formally 'educated' classes of society, rather than a sense of intellectual inferiority which is often a powerful force inhibiting the generation of confidence in the disadvantaged to rely on and assert their own thinking and take their own initiatives for development.

It is possible to acquire social knowledge without literacy, through methods of verbal enquiry and communication. But in many contexts not being literate amounts to surrendering power to literates, who claim knowledge which the disadvantaged cannot verify. Illiterate people depend on the literate for much information, as well as for dealings with public and other agencies which require the use of written instruments. Such dependence produces a sense of helplessness *vis à vis* institutions and structures which use the written language, and is liable to have powerful adverse effects on self-confidence in situations where relations with such institutions and structures are an important element of normal life and development effort of the people.

At the same time, the mode of acquiring literacy can have a significant bearing on the development or otherwise of self-confidence in the disadvantaged. A vertical mode of learning from conventional teachers coming from the more privileged social classes can perpetuate a sense of inferiority *vis à vis* the teachers and their social classes, who are regarded as the repository of knowledge and wisdom. As the teachings of Paulo Freire make very clear, literacy, or for that matter education as an element of social development, must be viewed as an organic component of a process of 'awakening' or 'animation' (Tilakaratna 1985). This implies not merely learning, knowing and understanding, but also experiencing and grasping one's own intellectual powers in the same process; to experience, in other words, self-discovery including the discovery of oneself as a thinker and creator of knowledge. This is what makes literacy a qualitative rather than a quantitative process.

3 *Self-reliance*: People's power comes ultimately from self-reliance. Self-reliance is not the same thing as self-sufficiency, but a combination of material and mental strength by which one can deal with others as an equal, and assert one's self-determination. Once again, any degree of control over material resources is by itself no indication of self-reliance, which is an attitudinal quality, inborn in some and acquired by others by social experience, social awareness, and reflection. Self-reliance is strengthened by a collective identity, deriving not only material strength but also mental strength from solidarity, sharing, and caring for each other, and from thinking and acting together to move forward and to resist domination.

Elements of organic development

Once empowered with organisation, social awareness, and a sense of self-reliance, people develop a collective personality. This development is an organic process; a question of the internal unfolding and progressive maturing of the collective. External agents may assist in this process of development; but a people cannot be developed by others. Some of the elements of people's development are suggested below.

Development of creativity

What distinguishes the human from other species is that human creativity is dynamic, seeking ever new forms of expression, fundamentally to fulfil a permanent creative urge; whereas other species at best create static structures (for example, a bird's nest) primarily for subsistence. The development of creative abilities and their fulfilment in economic, social, and cultural spheres is perhaps the most basic element of human development.

Institutional development

As a people's collective develops, it creates institutions and progressively modifies or recreates them, in order to manage collective affairs. The quality of institutional development in the context of their respective functions is one measure of people's development. This quality may in particular be assessed from the point of view of three basic functions for which institutional development is necessary. The first is the *management of collective tasks*, a self-evident function. The second is *mass participation* in collective deliberation and decision-making, in the implementation of collective tasks, in the taking of initiatives, in the review and evaluation of collective activities and of social progress. This is the question of internal democracy in collective development, to ensure both that activities are undertaken according to mass priorities and consensus, and that the wider body of people have sufficient opportunity to fulfil themselves by active participation in the activities of the collective. The third function, *solidarity*, is the one perhaps most neglected in conventional thinking. For sustained development, a collective needs to have mechanisms which will ensure that conflicts and tensions are handled without rupture; that people care for each other in distress (an internal social insurance function); and that some elements of the body do not develop at the expense of other elements so as to retard the process of development for them. There must be an agreed concern to avoid such 'mal-development', a mechanism for collective deliberation if such mal-development occurs or threatens to occur, and procedures for correcting the course.

Women's development

This cannot be overemphasised in view of the almost universal phenomenon of male development at the expense of women's development. The question is complicated by culture and religious beliefs in many situations where exogenously conceived norms of gender equality may not be appropriate. However, progress towards a position where women are able to articulate and assert their own points of view concerning gender relations in all spheres, and the evolution of gender relations towards greater equality as assessed by the women themselves, may be suggested as an important indicator of social development. For most societies this implies independent organisations for women, at least at the primary level.

Development of organic knowledge

The development of a collective human personality involves not only doing things, but also advancing simultaneously the analytical understanding of the evolving situation in all its dimensions — social, technological, political, and cultural. This is necessary for an intellectual appreciation of the unfolding experience, as well as to establish guidelines for future action, based on systematically experienced knowledge. In most societies the task of systematically developing such knowledge has become separated from the actual evolution of social life, and has become concentrated in the hands of professionals who by and large live a life very different from the lives of the ordinary people. For social development this has created the question of the relevance of much of the knowledge thus developed, which is not rooted in people's lives, and it has also contributed to retarding the process of development of the people by undermining popular knowledge and their ability to create and advance knowledge. While professional knowledge of some kinds remains valuable for social development at certain levels of decision making, the development of self-knowledge by the people as an organic part of their life's activities — organic knowledge — is perhaps more valuable. This organic knowledge helps to develop knowledge more immediately relevant for people's self-development, as well as for sustaining people's power to assert themselves *vis à vis* other social sectors. Organic knowledge, therefore, must be underlined as an important indicator of social development.

Social development of the wider society

For the broader society or a development programme of macro dimensions, social development means not only that grassroots people's organisations develop in the ways suggested above, but also that society as a whole develops, revealing essentially the same kind of qualitative features on a broader scale of operation or relations. Thus, concepts of self-reliance, social creativity, institutional development, capability for the management of broader social operations, democracy and solidarity are as much pertinent for assessment of social development for the wider society as for grassroots development. From the point of view of the status of the broad masses of people in overall social development, three desirable principles may be emphasised.

Human dignity

All people are entitled to human dignity, irrespective of economic status, ethnic origin, colour, or caste. A society has little claim to have developed where some sections can offend or abuse the human dignity of others and get away with it by virtue of their social power and position. One has not developed fully as a person, I would suggest, if one does not consider an offence to the human dignity of any person to be an offence to one's own dignity; without this basic identity with the human race one is not human oneself.

Popular democracy

At the level of institutional social discourse, an essential indicator of social development must be progress towards genuine popular democracy: a system whereby the broad masses of the people have an effective voice in the shaping of macro policy and in the conduct of public affairs. Neither the democracy of the so-called free world nor that of the so-called socialist democracies has ensured this natural right of the people. The nature of effective political parties and the outcome of electoral processes to determine macro-leadership of societies in the free world are critically determined by the distribution of economic power, and the economically underprivileged masses merely have the choice of influencing which set of privileged elites will rule over them. On the other hand, in socialist countries, albeit with greater economic equality, the Party remains typically unaccountable to the people. By one guise or another, in either type of society the real macro power remains in the hands of privileged elites. In this context, the entry of Solidarity of Poland, a truly workers' party, on to the stage of power is a so-far unique event that opens up the possibility in at least one modern society of a real sharing of power between privileged elites and the working people. If this possibility becomes truly fulfilled, and working people find a real voice in the affairs of the state, then the standard of attainable democracy and for that matter of macro-social development will have reached a new height, against which claims to democracy by other states, of both the free and the socialist worlds, could well be assessed.

Cultural diversity

Finally, in recent years we have witnessed an upsurge of assertions by popular sectors of their cultural identities, in opposition to attempts by dominant powers to impose a monolithic culture or ideology of development upon the people. In debates on individual vs. collective ownership of property, it is hardly even recognised that many indigenous people do not have the concept of humans *owning* natural resources such as land and water. Many such communities have instead the concept of humans *relating to* nature as a partner in life (offering the rest of us a model for the preservation of nature for 'sustainable' development, rather than its destruction to satisfy the human lust for acquisition and conquest).

Conclusion

Social development, from the point of view of the broader society, necessarily implies people's development at the grass roots; otherwise only the abstract concept of the 'nation state' would be promoted, and little else would develop except structures for manipulation and repression. People's development in its turn implies development with a people's authentic culture, which itself would develop in the process, absorbing elements from other cultures with which it would interact but which cannot develop by the imposition of alien cultures. A healthy developing society would, therefore, be a society that encourages the authentic development of people's cultures, to interact with each other for mutual enrichment, rather than in a bid for domination.

2.2 Qualitative dimensions of social development evaluation: Review of workshop papers and discussion

Introduction

The working group on qualitative indicators began its discussion by reviewing the present state of evaluation. It suggested that this was characterised by an excessive desire to quantify, by assumptions about people's behaviour and activities which were not supportable, by the often tenuous relationship between the results of an evaluation and what actually was happening, and by the relatively short time that evaluators spent with projects, which severely limited their ability to come to grips with what was really happening at the project level. Furthermore traditional forms of external, quantitative evaluation had introduced new forms of status difference within the spectrum of donor-project relations, and this had provoked increasing unease at the project level. It had also led to some distortion and consequent devaluing of the results of evaluation, and had introduced an overriding sense that project staff were being tested and found deficient.

The working group also discussed the general issue of evaluation from the point of view of the different actors involved in the process: funders, project staff, and local people. All evaluations are coloured by this kaleidoscope of actors, interests and interpretations. The actors all approach evaluation from different perspectives, and have different expectations of its outcome. In this respect, therefore, it is important to ask what does qualitative evaluation mean for these different actors? Project staff and local people may well see qualitative evaluation more in terms of illustrating the political dimensions of project activities; donor agencies, on the other hand, may be less enthusiastic and may prefer to insist upon quantitative data and information. Certainly there currently exists a general consensus that quantitative indicators are better able to evaluate project performance, and this consensus is a fundamental hurdle that qualitative evaluation faces.

The working group extended its opening discussion into the broad area of social development, its meaning and its characteristics. It concluded that social development is essentially a dynamic process directed towards building up the organisational base of poor people in order to give them some power to intervene in the development process. Social development is also to do with the satisfaction of human needs of all kinds: for emotional fulfilment, for democratic rights, for freedom to form political parties, and the right to participate in national life. In this respect, and although the workshop would be concentrating on the programme and project level, qualitative indicators of social development at the national level were also important. At both the national and local levels, social development is to do with changing the nature and balance of *power relations*, and all indicators of social development must reflect this dynamic relationship. In this respect it has to be recognised that not only governments but also NGOs are part of these power relations, although they may operate at different levels and also have different perceptions of the importance of these power relations in development.

A general framework for the working group's opening discussion was provided by Martin's paper, which was less concerned with the detail of qualitative indicators of social development as such; it used the case study of food aid in Peru and Colombia to illustrate not only the misuses of social development programmes but also the political sensitivity of the evaluation of such programmes. In such food aid programmes, Martin argued, such qualitative indicators as *power, control* and *self-sustainability* should be employed; but, because of their political sensitivity, few food aid evaluations use such indicators. Furthermore the evaluation of social development programmes like food aid should consider the international context of power relations between donor and recipient countries. In practice this never happens. Martin's paper further ranged over a number of key issues: the longer-term consequences of food aid, as opposed to its immediate effect; the potential conflict between the political and economic objectives of the donor agency and the supposedly developmental objectives of the programme; the consequences of food aid programmes for the target population; and the crucial issue of people's power as central to social development. Martin concluded that, whatever the nature or content of a social development programme, its validity will depend upon whether poor people have participated both in the process of social transformation and in the evaluation of programme consequences.

Issues relating to qualitative indicators

In both the papers presented to the working group and in the group's discussion, a whole range of issues was raised which touched upon the central theme of the identification and characterisation of qualitative indicators of social development. In the first instance it was suggested that qualitative indicators emerge as a result of an *interactive process* in which the local people would be involved; this is a *consensual* process, and not one that can be dictated by an external evaluator. Qualitative indicators emerge from the social development process itself and must be consistent with the social and cultural context in which the programme is operating. While on the basis of recent cumulative experience it is possible to make suggestions of possible qualitative indicators, blueprints or models cannot be used. The identification of relevant qualitative indicators for the evaluation of any social development programme is wholly and indisputably linked to the context and characteristics of that programme. The issues related to qualitative indicators raised by the papers and working group are summarised below.

1 Qualitative indicators of social development will almost certainly be derived from an analysis of change based upon existing and changing *power relationships.* Social development, by definition, implies a challenge to existing bases of power and its distribution, and a re-alignment of this power in favour of the powerless. The identification of qualitative indicators, therefore, should begin with a detailed analysis of power and its distribution within the project context; indicators could then be derived from the changing nature and characteristics of this power. Characteristics such as the control of local landowners, people's exclusion from discussion and debate on local development initiatives, or people's unwillingness or even fear to take action, for example, could form the basis of relevant indicators.

2 Central to the question of qualitative indicators is the issue of *development values.* Values become more crucial in the assessment of the qualitative aspects of development since, in the absence of fixed and tangible criteria, they help to construct a framework by which to judge progress. Values are also critical in terms of characterising such qualitative concepts as 'democratic rights', 'local participation', 'power sharing' and 'leadership', all of which can be found as qualitative objectives of social development. The way in which a person characterises and values a process of 'local participation' will be the basis upon which he or she identifies indicators relevant to the process. Values are at the heart of the way people interpret and evaluate activities in their immediate context, and the potentially conflicting values of the actors involved in social development will need to be taken into account in identifying appropriate qualitative indicators.

3 The determination of what could constitute a qualitative indicator of social development will be largely determined by the *varying perspectives of the agency or people involved.* These perspectives will differ in terms of needs, which in turn will determine what it is that should be evaluated. Donor agencies funding a process of social development, development agencies supporting the process, and local people experiencing the development occurring may all have different ideas of what indicators could be used in order to understand what is taking place. Qualitative indicators, therefore, must incorporate these various perspectives and not merely be left to an external evaluator to determine.

4 In most instances, qualitative indicators of social development cannot be predetermined and pre-packaged, but can only result from a process of *internal programme discussion.* An essential first stage in social development evaluation, therefore, is the internal process whereby commonly agreed indicators are identified. Such an approach has radical implications for conventional evaluations with externally designed instruments. Similarly such an exercise must be built into programme activities; the identification of relevant indicators must begin at the start of the programme and be modified and redefined over time. It will be difficult, if not impossible, to attempt in conventional *ex post* fashion to identify indicators after a programme has already run for a period of time.

5 Qualitative evaluation inevitably raises issues concerning the *objectivity* of the indicators used. Claims concerning the objectivity of conventional quantitative evaluation practice, in which indicators are normally determined on the basis of the conceptual framework and values of the external evaluator, can be challenged. Qualitative evaluation is concerned with those aspects of a development process in which the conceptual framework employed is critical to determining the nature of the change which has taken place. Qualitative indicators, therefore, cannot be solely externally determined, but must involve those who are directly experiencing the process of change. The indicators must be subjective to the people involved and based upon their interpretation, understandings and vocabulary. *Subjectivity* is the key to indicators which are both authentic and relevant, and this subjectivity can be achieved only by the local people who are experiencing the change taking place.

6 Finally it will be most difficult to talk in terms of models or blueprints of social development indicators. Since social development indicators will be essentially derived from the social and political context in which a programme is operating, it will be impossible to determine the indicators for any particular programme beforehand. The social and political contexts of local development are so varied throughout the Third World that the emphasis must be upon determining locally relevant indicators and not upon the imposing of dubious global ones. Social development indicators must be context-specific, and not merely plucked from some existing check-list or guidelines.

The working group also raised the question of how far we could distinguish between *conditions* and *indicators* of social development, or whether they were one and the same thing? As an example, the group took the issue of participation and asked whether people's participation was an essential indicator, or rather whether it was an essential condition of social development? The group concluded that the two were closely inter-related: what are seen as essential conditions of authentic social development, for example people's participation or a functioning people-based organisation, will in effect be the indicators to 'evaluate' the process. The identification of these 'essential conditions' of social development should inevitably lead to the identification also of relevant indicators.

Papers presented to the working group

Apart from Martin's paper, the two more substantial papers considered by the working group were presented by Harding and Robinson.

Philip Harding: 'Qualitative Indicators and the Project Framework'

This paper is based upon the author's work with the Overseas Development Administration, UK, and particularly with projects to improve slum conditions in three Indian cities. Harding's paper essentially argued that advocates of the 'project framework' approach to development must recognise the need for both qualitative and quantitative indicators when evaluating projects, and he explored this central argument with case study material from India. Specifically Harding asked the question whether, and to what extent, it is possible to incorporate qualitative indicators into the project framework style of project planning, and what form these indicators might take.

Harding elaborated upon the project framework approach and showed how, by bringing together both the 'wider' and 'immediate' objectives of a project, a more complete understanding of project impact is achieved. This project framework approach is, in Harding's opinion, useful in ensuring as complete an understanding as possible of the effect of project inputs and of overall quantifiable results; more complicated is its use in what Harding termed the 'process' project. Process projects are a response to the failure of the 'blueprint' approach to accommodate people-focused projects adequately. Process projects also usually involve beneficiaries in their design and implementation, and contain objectives which are less amenable to quantification. For example, Harding argued that in the context of the Indian Slum Improvement Project it is impossible to evaluate the impact of community development solely with numbers. The incorporation of qualitative indicators, however, into the project framework approach confronts two major barriers: for one thing, assessment is likely to be regarded as 'subjective' by project managers, as the criteria for measuring performance become a matter of individual choice; for another, the presentation of the results of qualitative assessment challenges the conventional format — graphs, tables and charts — used in the presentation of findings to project management.

The qualitative indicator: Indian slum improvement project

One of the objectives of the slum projects is to integrate the slum and its population into the life of the city. The upgrading of physical infrastructure within the slums does this in a physical sense. The inclusion of the incidence of marriage between slum dwellers and non-slum dwellers serves the purpose of providing an indicator of socio-economic integration. Likewise the incidence of neighbourhood/ bustee committees raising sufficient funds to employ the *balwadi* teacher, thus taking over responsibility from the implementing agency or NGO, can be taken as an indication of the value attached to education by the slum population and evidence of changes in slum dwellers' attitudes towards education.

The point here is that the creation of an objectively verifiable indicator does not turn a qualitative assessment into a quantitative one, even if some quantification is involved. An indicator which is measurable is necessary for the presentation of results in the project framework type approach. This is particularly so in projects such as those to do with the Indian slums where managers are dealing with processes taking place in a number of different locations. The social development adviser's task in this context is to identify other qualitative indicators which can then be objectified and assessed for the purposes of monitoring and evaluation. For example:

1 the regularity of meetings and the numbers attending, taking account of gender difference/age groupings; and

2 evidence that the contracts drawn up between the neighbourhood/ bustee committee and the implementing agency are being adhered to.

Such qualitative indicators could be taken together and the effectiveness of neighbourhood/bustee committees assessed in terms of their scored performances in these two areas or more. The results can then be presented in quantifiable form for the purposes of management, i.e. 70 per cent of committees are now functioning effectively, whereas only 20 per cent were previously so functioning.

Another example is provided by youth activities — and it will be noted that in none of the project frameworks are youth activities specifically mentioned as an indicator. The existence of youth groups in a slum indicates that there is potential for meeting the needs of the slum's young people. However, as with neighbourhood committees, we need indicators through which to assess their effectiveness in doing this. Similar indicators to those suggested for neighbourhood committees might be used. What is more, the interaction of slum youth groups with non-slum youth groups could be used as a further indicator of the socio-economic integration of the slum population into the life of the wider area. Indicators of integration might include

— the regularity of such interaction,
— the kinds of activities involved, and
— the channels of communication through which such events were set up — at whose instigation.

As with effectiveness, so the integration dimension could be measured by scoring slum youth groups according to these variables. The results of these qualitative considerations — the effectiveness of youth groups and their role in integrating slum youth into the life of the city — could be quantified for presentation to managers, i.e. that youth groups in 20 slums were achieving these on the previous visit and now youth groups in 28 slums are currently achieving these objectives.

(Harding 1989:6-8)

Harding stressed the exploratory nature of his work to date in relation to qualitative indicators and the Indian Slum Improvement Project, and stated that he saw the exploration as ongoing. He concluded that the qualitative indicator can be used within the context of the project framework approach and that furthermore, by building qualitative objectives into this approach from the beginning, the problem of subjectivity can be overcome. However, Harding still left unresolved the relationship between quantitative and qualitative indicators; indeed he argued that 'the fact that an indicator is eventually quantified does not disqualify it from being a qualitative indicator'. The quantification of the qualitative aspects of social development projects is still demanded by project management and, until this hurdle can be negotiated, it will be difficult to make any substantial conceptual breakthrough in the project framework approach to the qualitative evaluation of social development.

Mark Robinson: 'Performance Criteria in NGO Poverty Alleviation Programmes'

This paper examined the more conventional criteria of programme performance within the context of NGO-supported programmes. It was derived from a broader research programme looking in general terms at the relative effectiveness of NGO-supported development programmes. The focus of the paper was the identification of a number of key criteria and an examination of their relevance in the evaluation of the non-economic objectives of NGO-supported programmes. Robinson was concerned with poverty-alleviation programmes, seeing such programmes not just in terms of their economic impact but also in terms of their broader, qualitative impact on social development. He identified four criteria and assessed each from the standpoint of their use in evaluating these non-economic objectives.

1 *Effectiveness*: 'The degree by which an NGO programme or project's objectives are being achieved, measured against the resource costs incurred in achieving them.' Programme effectiveness is a measure of performance principally concerned with goal attainment and, in its measurement, linked to programme objectives. Robinson reviews a number of examples of the interpretation of 'effectiveness' in programme evaluation but, more importantly, he refers to an EEC study which concluded that, while the evaluation of project effectiveness is comparatively straightforward in theory, difficulties arise when the criterion is applied to social development projects. In such projects objectives are often not clearly stated at the outset, but developed over the course of implementation; similarly such projects often do not have clear physical targets, which further complicates any assessment of effectiveness. Input-output effectiveness of social development projects, therefore, is not easy to measure by tangible criteria.

2 *Efficiency:* Efficiency refers to the rate at which inputs are converted into outputs in the form of programme or project impact. More commonly efficiency is measured through cost-benefit analysis, by assigning numerical values to inputs and outputs. The question which Robinson raised is whether, even when modified as social cost-benefit analysis, this is an appropriate tool for measuring social development projects. Two problems exist: first, few NGO-supported small development projects produce the kind of reliable baseline or longitudinal data for cost-benefit analysis; and, second, the measurement of benefits from a project cannot be undertaken with great accuracy unless a project has narrowly conceived or technical objectives, which is not the case with social development projects. Generally Robinson argued the case for the use of cost-benefit analysis 'in broad terms rather than with mathematical precision', but stressed the problem of assigning weights to non-quantifiable benefits, in that numerical values for such benefits may well be derived from the subjective assessment of project success.

3 *Impact:* Impact is associated with the broader consequences of a development project and therefore goes beyond the direct benefits arising from the intervention itself. Robinson suggested that there is a range of possible indicators which can be used to determine impact: economic, social, technical and environmental indicators, for example. The precise list of indicators would depend very much on the type of project being evaluated. In terms of the impact of social development projects, Robinson identified from the practice a number of possible indicators: *increased capacity for self-organisation, higher literacy rates, improved status of women* and *reduced dependence on landlords or patrons,* for example.

4 *Sustainability:* Sustainability, or viability, refers to the longer-term continuation of a project following withdrawal of external support. The centrality of sustainability in evaluating project performance is now being acknowledged; both the recognised shortcomings of static cost-benefit analysis in assessing longer-term viability, and the importance of 'benefit continuation' in projects designed to promote sustained improvements support this centrality. Robinson argued, for example, that where a social development project emphasises 'empowerment' and 'community organisation', it is unlikely that the more concrete results of a project will become apparent if project momentum is not sustained. NGO project experience to date has shown that such factors as *local resource availability, the quality of community participation,* and *local institutional development,* for example, can be important indicators of the degree of sustainability.

Measuring project impact

A USAID-sponsored evaluation of NGO projects in Kenya and Niger applied the cost-benefit approach in examining development impact, which was defined broadly to include direct benefits generated as a result of NGO resources, a sustained flow of benefits after withdrawal of the external agency, and prospects for future development in related activities. A cost-benefit ratio was calculated for each project based on 'monetised' (ie. quantifiable) benefits; 'in kind' (direct, but non-quantifiable) benefits were recorded but not entered into the calculation. A scoring system was utilised to assess various factors contributing to sustainability and replication, and combined with the cost-benefit ratios relating to direct benefits, in order to draw overall conclusions on impact.

(Robinson 1989)

Robinson concluded his paper by recognising the difficulties concerning data and the evaluation of non-economic benefits:

The problem here is essentially one of interpretation rather than of enumeration. Where the aim is to identify qualitative factors contributing to successful interventions, the approach will have to be capable of generating insights on a project's worth which are verifiable by others, rather than simply the predispositions of individual evaluators.

The research continues!

Suggested qualitative indicators of social development

The working group concluded its discussion by seeking to identify appropriate qualitative indicators of social development. In the first instance it was agreed that these indicators can only come out of an intensive process of internal discussion between participants and project staff. A decision which is reached through internal negotiation about which are the most appropriate indicators will help both to ensure the indicators' relevance and also that participants understand and can be involved in the evaluation exercise. In identifying appropriate indicators the working group suggested that two basic stages were involved: first the identification of key areas of activity of social development which might provide appropriate indicators and, second, specific indicators which could be used to identify, characterise, and 'measure' changes in these key areas. In the first instance the working group suggested the following as a series of areas which could provide the basis for appropriate qualitative indicators:

— More general access for poor people to the resources necessary for development; greater distribution of resources available.
— Greater expression of self-identity by poor people, and the right to full involvement in national life.
— Movement towards greater social equality, measured through the strengthening of non-hierarchical relationships among poor people.
— Improved levels of caring and concern for others at national level.
— Overall improvements in physical wellbeing and security.
— Reduction of dependency relationships among poor people.
— The development of organisational capacity among poor people.
— The creation of awareness.

These do not constitute a definite series of areas, nor a model for the evaluation of social development. Their purpose essentially is to help break down the overall concept of social development into a series of areas of potential change which can be used as a guide in an evaluation exercise. They will help us to answer the question 'What could have been the effect or impact of a particular social development programme?' Each of the above criteria is expressed in general terms, and will need to be interpreted more carefully within the context within which the programme is operating. The series of areas constitute in effect a framework for reference in considering the issue of social development evaluation. This is how the series should be used and refined in terms of the context of the social development programme being evaluated.

The next and more detailed stage in the process is the identification of relevant indicators which would illustrate the above areas of change and form the basic structure of the evaluation exercise. Here the working group commented that the identification of such indicators would need further time and research. This more detailed stage could best be done by a smaller workshop concentrating solely on the practice of qualitative evaluation at the project level. Such an exercise would help isolate the conceptual framework of the qualitative evaluation of social development — which essentially has been the theme of this workshop — from an analysis of the methods and techniques of this form of evaluation.

In its report, however, the working group presented several examples of the kinds of indicators which would need to be identified. Indicators which give information on *group characteristics* might be derived from an analysis of the nature of participation in group meetings and activities, from an analysis of emerging feelings about group purpose and solidarity, from an appreciation of awareness about issues and problems, or from an understanding of the enthusiasm and support for group activities that exists. Indicators which give information about *self-reliance* might be found from a study of how meetings are organised and how dependency on outsiders is reduced. Indicators of *independence* might be derived from an analysis of organisational growth and the establishment of alliances and networks with other organisations. Finally the working group suggested a number of project level indicators which could be relevant:

— evidence of *shared decision making* among participants and project staff
— signs of *commitment* among participants to the project group's goals and activities
— evidence of *shared leadership* among project group participants
— signs of *solidarity* and *cohesion* among the project group
— improving level of *technical and managerial competence* among project group participants
— capacity for self-reflection and critical analysis among participants
— collective capacity of the project group to undertake *action* in response to problems identified.

The working group stressed that the above were presented as examples of the kinds of indicators which would have to be developed at the project; they did not constitute an authoritative checklist, nor were they necessarily universally applicable.

The working group concluded its discussions by stressing that in project evaluation, the responsibility of project groups to the donor agencies remains implicit. It is the donor agency which usually initiates the demand for evaluation, and the indicators suggested often reflected a particular world view and particular requirements. Such views and requirements should be negotiated with project participants *before* being incorporated as reliable and appropriate indicators. These negotiations should take place at the planning stage, rather than during the execution of a particular project, and they should be focused on the agency, rather than on the project. Indicators should be based upon the internally perceived realities of the project, and not upon the desk-orientated demands of the external agency.

Papers submitted to the working group on the qualitative dimensions of social development evaluation

Judi Aubel: 'Notes on the Issue of Qualitative Indicators'

Philip Harding: 'Qualitative Indicators and the Project Framework'

Gonzalo Martin: 'Notes on the Evaluation of Social Development Projects and Programmes in the Third World'

Mark Robinson: 'Performance Criteria in NGO Poverty Alleviation Programmes'

SECTION 3

THE METHODOLOGY OF SOCIAL DEVELOPMENT EVALUATION

3.1 The methodology of social development evaluation: Thematic paper

Ignacio Garaycochea

Introduction

Theoretical and practical aspects of social development evaluation are largely determined by the different interpretations ascribed to social development. In an explicit or implicit way, governments, social development researchers, donor agents, local intermediaries, evaluators, and beneficiaries have a particular understanding of what social development is. To some extent, these different interpretations lead to different modes of putting social development into practice and therefore on how to evaluate it. Under these circumstances it would be difficult to pose one single methodology for the evaluation of social development projects.

However many particular differences might exist in the interpretation of social development, there has been a growing effort in the past decade to assemble them within a broader understanding. Social development is regarded as a process in which the sectoral and holistic aspects of development move forward and maintain a correspondent relation. At this point we could argue over the methodology of evaluating social development projects as 'a process within a process'. Processes need to be described and interpreted as they occur over time, as qualitative and quantitative events, in order to gain a complete view of the social effect caused by project intervention. The evaluation of qualitative objectives (for example, participation, solidarity or popular education) represents a particular area of interest when looking at social development projects and programmes.

One of the key elements when considering strategies for social development evaluation is the relationship between the concept and its operational dimension. How social development is understood or conceived will have in turn an effect on how it is put into practice, and therefore how it should be evaluated. There is a vast body of literature on the concept of social development, though still few commonly shared definitions are to be found. We would prefer to think in terms of more than one concept (even sub-concepts) related to the definition of social development. These interpretations can go from the more tangible activities, such as provision of health and educational services, to a type of intervention that is non-tangible and therefore unable to be given a numerical value, such as the development of political awareness among peasants.

At field level we find that most practitioners of social development have their own interpretations and ideas on matters that are closely linked with its practice. Commonly this is perceived as a divorce between the theoretical aspects of social development, in which the academic is more involved, and the daily aspects as experienced by a development worker at field level. (It would not be unrealistic to think that social development is in itself a practical or a living concept.)

Social development is better expressed as a process in which multi-dimensional activities, particular and general, take place in both quantitative and qualitative terms. As we noted before, some interpretations of social development tend to weigh more on the quantitative side, while others give more emphasis to the qualitative side. This in turn has a relevance when setting the project's objectives and ways to implement it. At the end of the day a project's particular orientation will have an effect on the methodology of evaluation. (What to evaluate? How to evaluate? For whom?) A particular concern of social development evaluation is to evaluate the non-productive or non-material objectives in a given project (for example, self-reliance, popular education, or upgrading cultural features).

Social development as a process

To evaluate social development means to evaluate a process, that is to say, to understand the process which unfolds when intervention has taken place. If evaluatory exercises are integrated in a social development process, they become part of it. Thus, the methodology of evaluation becomes part of the project's general strategy. It is not concerned as an isolated or external element in an organic body; it is more like a 'process within a process' situation. Compared to traditional forms of evaluation (cost-benefit analysis), social evaluation does not conclude in a specific 'canned' product, because it has the nature of being simultaneously an output and an input contained in a continuous process.

Some of the major difficulties that social development projects face are the processes and the qualitative objectives they pursue. In fact, the 'difficulty with objectives such as participation is not only that they are difficult to characterize, but also that it is not possible at the beginning of a project to predict what the outcome or effect might be' (Oakley 1988:5). In addition to this, the results of the project could not be visible during its life span or by the time it has finished. Effects can appear later in the future, and in a context where we will not be able to determine to what extent changes or actions taking place are due to the project's past intervention.

Another issue related to this topic is to ask to what extent project members have control of the processes taking place in it. We might know when and how to switch on the mechanisms to start a social development process, but we do not know when and where it is going to finish. Social development projects are dynamic and do not necessarily follow a predetermined direction. We should take into account that social development projects can develop unexpected results. Even though a project might not accomplish its initial goals (the predetermined parameters against which evaluation is supposed to rest) the project can still be a success. This is the case with a Peruvian Social Forestry Project (described in detail below), of which one of the objectives was to create an environmental consciousness among Andean peasants in order to preserve the ecological balance of the area. However, the project's methodology of intervention/reflection/action enabled peasants to realise that among their priorities, the strengthening of communal organisations was something more important to do, though they did not disregard the ecological issues.

When we describe and interpret processes taking place in a social development project there are two distinct dimensions of where to look for the attainment of objectives: the collective or group processes and the individual or personal processes and changes. How to detect and describe these features through evaluation is a major task in the arena of social development.

Donor agents, evaluators and social development evaluation

There is a time in the life of most social development projects (particularly those of NGOs) when they are prompted by donor agents to undertake an evaluation. When examining the donor agent's perspective on evaluation, it is possible to sense an underlying desire for accountability. In this case the particular purpose of evaluation is associated with the future funding of the project, or the need to channel financial resources to the right project. The methodology of evaluation is very much biased by donor agents towards the quantitative aspects of social development. Development workers are generally urged by the donor agent to present some kind of reliable evidence on how the project is evolving and how objectives are being reached. Usually this type of reliability or credibility is based upon the measurement of the degree of confidence in the progress of the project and is related to 'the number' as the neutral or objective element for evaluation. Conventional evaluation is very prone to use a type of methodology that emphasises the quantitative aspects of a process, and more particularly the economic side of a project. For this, cost-benefit analysis (CBA) has long become the most commonly used technique to evaluate development projects.

Many evaluators of social development have to confront the dilemma of whose needs the evaluation is going to satisfy. Thus, the methodology for evaluation is also shaped at this level and according to the demands of both interested parties: the donor agent, who is usually interested in the quantitative aspects, and the project holder, who is more concerned with the qualitative side. The methodological approach to these two types of evaluative requests is met through a 'double-purpose methodology' that manages to combine the quantitative and the qualitative objectives of social development. The issue of accountability is also often brought by the donor agent and with a pressure that distorts the value of quantitative indicators. However, it does not mean that in a self-financed project the accountable dimension will disappear in order to pay more attention to the qualitative aspects. Qualitative and quantitative measures are not mutually exclusive, and should co-exist in the evaluation process.

Indicators for social development evaluation

The evaluation of the qualitative aspects of social development projects, particularly non-material and non-directly productive objectives, represents a crucial issue in the growth of the social development process. The methodology to evaluate such a process calls for a new perspective. Qualitative evaluation is understood as being more concerned with describing the characteristics and properties of a process like participation over a period of time, and then with interpreting the data and information available in order to make statements concerning the nature and extent of the process which has occurred. Choosing appropriate indicators for the evaluation of qualitative aspects means to select an element or components within the social process that can best describe the same process. Political awareness, for example, cannot be measured by collecting and analysing numerical data, yet an indicator or a set of indicators is needed to depict and to explain phenomena taking place along the process.

Evaluating social development projects against an agreed objective (for example, awareness building or consciousness raising among women in a determined village) has proved to be of very limited use. It is difficult to predict how these objectives might manifest themselves and what their eventual nature might be. Moreover, these objectives are processes that are expected to surpass the life of a project; the attainment of an objective becomes a new input that enriches the social experience. Thus, consciousness raising is not an objective in itself, but just one link of the chain.

Since social development is concerned with every individual in society and no one should be neglected, social indicators are not meant to describe and interpret only the collective or group phenomena, but to take into consideration also the individual processes. Social creativity, self-reliance, or popular democracy must be described and explained at the group and individual levels if a complete understanding of the process is sought. However, it should be important to explore if indicators have a universal validity or pertinence for evaluation. Is it possible to use one type of indicator for the description of collective and individual processes? Would it be possible to make a particular inference from an indicator that provides the sources for a general assessment?

If methodology is going to be defined by a particular understanding or perspective of social development and the context in which the project operates, indicators must also have this flexible nature. Indicators for evaluating social development may be developed in the concrete context of the project or programme's specific objectives, its social and cultural aspects, and its development by the 'project community'.

Concluding comments

In the search for better ways to evaluate social development projects, what is important is to recognise the existence of more than one way to go about it. Social evaluation should be considered as a process within a process in which a suitable methodology can be tailored to fit project and contextual characteristics. Social, cultural and economic considerations of the project's internal and external milieux should help to mould the methodology. Indicators should be considered according to the expectations of the methodology just defined. The evaluative process is considered to be an educational experience in which 'communal' participation is highly desired, a learning process of knowing what it is we are evaluating and how to do it. Different perspectives of the same process can be obtained if different groups participate in the exercise: beneficiaries, neighbouring people, field workers, project staff, and external facilitators. Finally, what is important when evaluating social processes is to experience a sense and feeling of progress and change caused by people as masters of their destiny.

Evaluating social forestry in Peru: a case study

Introduction

The socio-forestry project Arbol Andino, in the southern Andes of Peru, is based on a methodology for promoting forestry among peasant communities that seeks to generate an environmental consciousness among these peasants. Pedagogic principles supporting this methodology and its implementation are based on Paulo Freire's reflection-action theory. Although the project considers that the reflection is initially oriented towards the forestry aspect, it could be extended in the medium term towards the everyday problems of peasants.

The project's methodology is implemented through the organisation of reflection groups within every community. Afterwards it is expected that the members of these groups will in turn generate a more general reflection within the rest of the community. The process of reflection is initiated and animated by a team of promoters trained by the project. During the whole process the extension agent is not considered as a technician who is going to educate peasants, but rather as an 'animador' or 'facilitator' of the process of conscientisation. This agent could be considered as a 'trainer of trainers', in as much as his or her activity principally takes place among the members of the reflection groups, who later work with the community.

The Arbol Andino project included as a part of its methodology of evaluation an external *ad hoc* evaluation team who could help make more objective the results produced by the internal evaluators. The external team was formed by an interdisciplinary-interethnic group who worked in 16 Aymara peasant communities for a period of four months. The team did not consider itself as a group of experts but rather as a catalyst in the reflection process.

The basic task of the evaluation was to examine the effects produced by the project with regard to:

— the change in attitudes of peasants faced with the problems of forestry degradation in their community;
— the increase in the peasants' capacity to analyse and solve the problems of their community, starting from the model of reflection suggested by the project.

By 'attitude' we understand the disposition of an individual to react in one way or another when faced with a problem or a certain question which is reflected in a set of opinions with respect to the mentioned subject that the individual may or may not express. To measure the change of attitude provoked among peasants by the project, we considered their opinions about the problem of forestry and closely related aspects. Here their opinions are seen as the verbal expression of their attitudes; we argue, therefore, that an opinion symbolises an attitude.

By 'capacity' we understand the ability developed by an individual to confront and resolve certain problems. This capacity is generated as a result of the conscientisation of the individual in relation to the problem and the analysis of surrounding limitations.

From the project's perspective, a favourable attitude towards forestry implies on the part of the peasant an equally favourable disposition to participate in an active manner in the activities of the project. A positive attitude towards the project assumes primarily a knowledge and secondly a receptivity to and understanding of its messages and propositions. With respect to the capacity to solve problems, this implies an ability to solve problems, and includes the individual and collective identification of appropriate solutions. The ability of peasants involved in the project to reflect upon issues and problems, therefore, is directly related to their analytical skills and their attitudes towards the taking of action.

The methodology of evaluation

The approach used, which was descriptive-analytical and interpretative, favoured the qualitative aspects of the evaluation. This approach was of particular help in the analysis of information collected at the community level, from different perspectives. A whole range of observations was made on the studied situation, in such a manner that all the personal 'subjective' appreciations could be compared, analysed and finally 'objectivised'. The methodology used included an element of comparative analysis between communities attended by the project and two communities outside the project area. The latter were situated in the same ecological zone as the project's communities. One of these other communities had been attended for several years by another forestry project, but the other until now had no experience with forestry projects whatsoever.

For the measurement of attitudes, the following procedures and techniques were employed:

a. Data collection: A form of structured interview was used. However, data were not collected on the basis of pre-determined categories, but rather there was a spontaneous codification of the gathered information, using categories determined by the interviewed peasants. In almost all the cases the interview was performed in the local language (Aymara). The required information was elicited also with the help of illustrations which provided the context for the interview, as well as a minimal input of information to make the interview possible. Interviews were sound-recorded and afterwards transcribed and translated into Spanish.

b. Systematisation and analysis: The information thus gathered was systematised at two different times. Firstly, the identification of categories was deduced from the answers of the interviewed people. Secondly, the categories were organised hierarchically, assigning numerical values, and from these, attitudinal scales were elaborated. Attitudinal scales were divided into five and three intervals, all identified with a certain value. Attitudinal scales were based on the ideological assumptions of the project. For example, an answer like 'we need to organise ourselves' was considered more close to the positive extreme of the scale than an answer like 'we need to plant trees', as the project aims to create an environmental conscientisation and not just stimulate the mechanical activity of planting trees. In order to be able to compare the different communities in which the project was functioning, it was necessary to determine the 'global attitude' of the interviewed peasants in every community, for which the respective answers obtained were summarised and put into the scales for every question formulated. From this result we obtained a qualified weighting from every individual and from every community, which permitted us to realise an average comparison between the communities.

For the measurement of the capacity to solve problems, the following procedures were employed:

a. Data collection: During the collection of information two complementary techniques were used: problem solving and role simulations. Through these combined activities it was the intention to evaluate the capacity of peasants to establish analogies and to apply to different situations the pedagogical steps learned during their participation in the project. This exercise was practised with the members of the reflection groups organised in each community. Peasants were given two days to complete the task they were assigned.

In the problem-solving exercise, pictorial aids were also used, in which a sequence of actions was described that together constituted a problematic situation affecting the community. Once the problem(s) had been identified, the group ws expected to establish appropriate alternative solutions. Afterwards, these alternatives had to be presented verbally as well as in written form before a simulated community assembly consisting of the evaluation team. However, on more than one occasion the presentation took place in front of the real community assembly in which a larger number of the peasants were present. Verbal presentations of the groups were recorded, and the written documents constituted important analytical material for the external evaluators.

b. Systematisation and analysis: The information obtained was systematised and analysed, based on the incorporated elements of the written works as well as the verbal expositions (simulated assemblies) produced by the peasants. In respect of the written works, these were examined for their form and content. Of particular importance was the observation of how peasants made use of and enriched their typical school knowledge and skills, to classify and to present in a visual manner the product of the group reflections and analysis. This exercise enabled peasants to discriminate between the essential and the secondary, and the anecdotal and the general, allowing them to extract the essence of their problems and express it in a written way. The different levels of complexity found in the contents of the written works presented by the group were reflected in their analysis. In this way written works were classified in three groups: simple, mixed, and complex forms.

Two proceedings were used in the analysis of verbal presentations (simulated assemblies). Firstly a matrix was established in order to define high-low degrees of the community's self-reliant initiative (implying the creativity to elaborate alternative solutions), and high-low degrees of dependency on relief agencies (which means a relapse of confidence when the support of institutions and projects is withdrawn). In the next stage categories of thought were elaborated, ranging from simple memory through systematisation, relation, deduction, and reflection to creativity.

Peasants in the reflection groups manifested a tendency towards creativity. In the control communities a lower tendency to generate proper alternatives was perceived, and a tendency towards external dependency was noted.

Concluding comments

For the evaluation of social projects, such as the one described here, there are no pre-determined methodological schemes. The methodology is tailored in relation to the project's surrounding context and its general scope. In the case of Arbol Andino, a number of issues should be noted:

— The project's evaluation strategy included the participation of an external team.
— The assumptions or starting points of the project as well as its objectives and goals.
— The cultural, social, economic, and educational aspects of the people involved within and outside the project.

The descriptive, interpretative, and analytical approach used in the evaluation proved to be adequate in terms of time and in relation to the quantity and quality of the information obtained. However it also favoured the collection of qualitative data; special efforts were then made to quantify and assess these qualitative data statistically. The different perspectives taken in the analysis of the qualitative data helped to make the analysis more objective. Furthermore the contrasting of 'with' and 'without' project situations was particularly useful as a means of measuring the changes taking place in peasants' participation in the project.

Establishing a rapid and close relation between peasants and the members of the evaluation team was possible, thanks to both sides' sensitivity and capacity for integration. The latter was largely due to the fact that some members of the team came from the same cultural context as the peasants.

3.2 The methodology of social development evaluation: Review of workshop papers and discussion

Introduction

In the context of Garaycochea's paper, the working group reviewed a number of other papers presented in the broad area of the methodology of evaluation of social development. (These papers are listed at the end of this chapter.) In general terms the working group emphasised the relationship between the conceptual framework for the evaluation of social development and the methodologies and instruments employed. The former clearly influences the latter, and indeed dictates the kinds of instruments and methodologies used. Similarly it was suggested that there is no one universally applicable methodology for the evaluation of social development, but rather a range of alternative approaches and elements which can be drawn upon in relation to the demands of the local context. Different constituencies will have different needs for evaluation, and the different actors at the different levels within the project community will each have different interests, which will have to be catered for in the methodologies employed.

The evaluation of social development does not take place within a vacuum, and it should be seen as an aid to development, rather than an instrument of control. Inevitably, before we get involved in the methodology of evaluation, we have to ask questions such as for whom is the evaluation intended, and why is an evaluation necessary? Methodology comes at the end of the evaluation process, and will be influenced by the kinds of issues — indicators, partnership, and the role of the evaluator — which are discussed elsewhere. The methodology of evaluation is the means whereby we link a series of potentially disjointed activities; how we build coherence into the evaluation exercise. The overall methodology of the evaluation exercise should be distinguished from the methodological techniques, for example, questionnaires, which may be used. The evaluation of social development should be first and foremost an educational as opposed to a managerial tool, and it should be seen as emerging from and reflecting methodologies implicit in social development as a process. Similarly the methodology of evaluating social development is not simply the methodology of social development, but a distinctive and separate aspect of the process as a whole. Evaluation is not an autonomous process, but its operation will demand its own approach and will use techniques and instruments relevant to the need to understand and document the process of social development.

Towards an alternative methodology

The evaluation of social development as a qualitative process of change leads us into a different paradigm of development thinking and action. Oakley's paper has reviewed the conceptual issues involved, and these in turn influence the nature of evaluation methodology. It must be said, however, that while perhaps we understand the limitations of conventional, quantitative evaluation methodology, we are still exploring and experimenting with relevant alternatives. Simply, we do not yet have proven and tested methodologies for the evaluation of the qualitative process of social development. For example, Sollis and Moser outlined a number of methodological alternatives which they considered in their work analysing the social costs of structural adjustment in Guayaquil, Ecuador: the use of key informants, the large-scale structured household survey, and techniques of rapid rural appraisal. They found that, while most were useful, they were inadequate for evaluating the key consumption patterns of respondents. Similarly King and Silkin, in outlining their approach to the evaluation of a Comprehensive Development Programme in Eritrea, found that indicators available were unable to reflect the 'social issues' related to the programme, and that questions linked to quantitative aspects inevitably drew prescriptive responses and failed to reveal the kinds of social transformations that might be taking place.

Several of the studies presented to the working group analysed the basis of a methodology of evaluation of social development and identified key issues. Inevitably, however, these issues were more related to the deficiencies of the more conventional, quantitative approach to evaluation; methodologies are emerging more as adjustments to inadequate, conventional practice than as proven and relevant alternatives. We can summarise the issues identified in several papers as follows:

1 Evaluation is inevitably seen as some kind of *outside* activity which must be done by donors and officials, rather than by the people themselves. *Control* of evaluation is critical, and it is normally assumed that control remains with the outside donors. Altafin, for example, linked this control to communication means used in evaluation and showed how outsiders determine the knowledge and the means of transference in evaluation exercises. Similarly Taylor concluded that outsiders were nearly always reluctant to transfer the impetus of evaluation to the members of the community.

2 Conventional methodologies of evaluation assume a *command of numbers and basic reading skills* (Uphoff). In this way the task of evaluation is taken out of the people's hands. Evaluation methodologies are required, therefore, which require no knowledge of arithmetic and only basic literacy skills.

3 Too often the evaluator is seen as a judge rather than a facilitator. Conventionally evaluators are expected to stand in objective assessment of a programme's outcome and to treat people as possible contributors of knowledge and ideas. *The evaluator as facilitator* is an entirely different role and demands different skills and techniques.

4 Since indicators are basic to any process of evaluation, *the determining of relevant indicators* is critical. Normally, however, indicators are externally determined and almost certainly not understood by local people. Uphoff reported upon research findings which showed that, where such indicators were externally determined, margins of error of up to 100 per cent could result, since respondents clearly did not understand the indicators used.

5 Conventional methodologies of evaluation are *standardised* and *inflexible*, and leave little space for local adaptation. Evaluations are previously prepared and ready to be put into practice. Furthermore, evaluation design takes little note of time and does not allow for the accompanying of a long- term process (Vargas). Such standardisation is acceptable in situations of common inputs and outputs, but is entirely inappropriate in the evaluation of qualitative processes.

6 Social development cannot always be understood in terms of expected and visible results; the dynamic of social development often leads to *unexpected results* which demand a form of evaluation not linked to predetermined parameters and indicators. The evaluation of social development, therefore, must be sensitive to these possible unexpected results and be able both to identify and to explain them.

In his proposals for an Alternative Methodology for the Evaluation of Social Development, David Brown emphasises the difficulties in measuring such qualitative processes as *empowerment* and suggests that 'oblique techniques' will have to be used; furthermore there are intrinsic problems in trying to use short-term techniques to measure long-term processes. Analysing social development in terms of a process of normative change, Brown highlights a number of inherent difficulties associated with the evaluation of normative change:

1   *Subjectivity*: the evaluator inevitably has his or her own values in relation to change in the attitudes and behaviour of the target population. These values are often masked by sophisticated theoretical argument, but nonetheless they constitute a problem of subjectivity.

2   *Arbitration*: while social development projects may claim to rest upon the participants' own understanding of the development occurring, there is a strong tendency for evaluations to draw heavily upon external interpretation of the changes involved.

3   *Positive bias*: the methodological instruments used in the evaluation of social development can strongly prejudice the evaluation process towards a positive observational bias, in which the group actors 'mirror' the attitudes of the change agents with whom they are in contact. Because the stated aims of the project are to create attitudinal changes, the evaluation process is prejudiced towards interpretations which favour explanations in these terms.

4   *Relationship to dominant ideologies*: the existing polarity between 'traditional' and 'modern' world views inevitably influences evaluation. The ideological context of a project will strongly permeate both its approach and its evaluation. This can result in evaluations functioning as a means to give theoretical validity to highly partisan attitudes, rather than as a means of objective assessment.

All contributors underlined the complex and potentially sophisticated nature of the evaluation of qualitative processes of development. In order to ensure that local people are put centre stage in any evaluation, there must be a reversal in the ways in which authority and evaluation control are seen at the project level. It was widely argued that local people should be in a position to define the terms and types of evaluation with which they wish to become involved, which they believe could evaluate their project's performance and over which they could have authorised control. While a coherent and common framework of principles for social development evaluation may not yet be emerging, what is agreed is that the dominant evaluation paradigm must be re-negotiated.

CAFOD-ERA: Evaluation of the Mogoraib regional comprehensive development programme

Since 1987 CAFOD [the Catholic Fund for Overseas Development] has been funding a five-year comprehensive development programme in the Mogoraib-Forto region of Eritrea, involving 4,000 households. The proposal of the Mogoraib-Forto Comprehensive Development Programme is to help the people of this area to increase their food production and improve rural services.

The terms of the funding agreement between CAFOD and the Eritrean Relief Association makes provision for a mid-term evaluation after Year 2. A formal evaluation is planned after the harvest of 1990 involving both CAFOD, ERA and representatives from the project steering committees. This evaluation will look for progressive indicators in environmental, technical, social, and economic baselines.

It was agreed that the same references used in the evaluation of the Rora Habab programme (a similar programme in another area) should be used for the evaluation of MRCDP, so that useful comparisons between the two regions could be made. However, the CAFOD evaluation team thought that the model of evaluation developed in Rora Habab did not sufficiently define social baseline indicators to analyse the social character of the area which could affect the project's success. Thus, it was agreed that a pre-social evaluation was to take place in Mogoraib to enable at least CAFOD, as the 'outsiders' in this process, to develop a better understanding of the social factors of the area and the part these play in the comprehensive development programmes of this kind.

The pre-social evaluation aimed to answer the question: What constraints are imposed on development in Mogoraib and Forto by the social composition and pattern of relations in each of the two sub-districts? In order to tackle this question a survey questionnaire was set up to examine intra- and inter-household relations in the project area. The survey covered questions related to household composition, household assets, non-farming household resources, the division of labour within the household, and economic and social links between households.

The evaluator, in consultation with the Steering Committee for the MFCDP, selected the villages in each of Mogaraib and Fort districts. The villages selected should have been surveyed by the 1987 Food Assessment Survey, to facilitate cross-data examination. Because of timing (14 days for the completion of the survey), only a small number of villages were selected. The sample chosen was representative of the various class and ethnic groups of each village.

The results of the evaluation were then presented in a variety of ways: in quantitative form (tables), qualitative form (case studies), outsider's and insider's views about the social structure, a detailed historical account of social change and development in Barka, and broader aspects of contemporary development in the area defined by cadres from the Department of Public Administration and members of the people's Committee. Appendices were attached to give further information: maps, tables of age/productivity ratio; and amount of availability and distribution of consumer goods.

(King and Silkin 1989)

Some experimental approaches

The papers under review present a wide range of examples of methodological approach to the evaluation of social development. Garaycochea's study above looks in detail at the issue of methodology in the context of a social forestry project in Peru. The other examples ranged from a highly systematised approach to evaluation as practised by the World Bank (McPhail) to a more detailed examination of the role of communication in such evaluations (Altafin). When we talk of methodology of evaluation, we are asking the question 'how?'. How do we go about evaluating processes such as social development? What is the approach we take, and what methodological tools can we employ? In answering this question, the papers presented ranged from the conceptual (Brown), to the anecdotal (Taylor), and more practical examples (Uphoff, Sollis and Moser).

All the examples were largely experimental in nature and confirmed that we are still feeling our way in terms of proven methodologies for the evaluation of social development. A basic issue running through all the examples is the quantitative-qualitative divide; whether the approach to evaluation should start from the solid basis of quantitative data and probe into the more qualitative aspects, or whether a qualitative approach should form the basis, supported as appropriate by quantitative data. At this moment there is no proven solution to this problem. The surer ground is to collect the information and data which are immediately available and seek to extrapolate qualitative outcomes from them; the more demanding and still unproven approach is to build the evaluation around the qualitative outcomes. Methodologically the two approaches are different, and this difference was reflected in the examples presented. Pulling together the range of methodological examples, however, and reviewing the varied discussions held, we noted that a number of key issues emerged which would need to be taken into consideration when structuring the evaluation methodology:

1   Essentially the methodology should be based upon the notion of *self-evaluation*, in which those directly involved in the qualitative process are instrumental in assessing its progress and outcomes. In this respect the evaluation becomes an 'inside', as opposed to an 'outside', activity. Methodologically, therefore, it is impossible to conceive of the evaluation of social development which is not rooted in the immediate participants, and where these participants do not have direct access to the different stages and instruments of the evaluation exercise.

2   The methodology should not be seen as a mechanical, dispassionate activity unrelated to the livelihoods of the project participants. The methodology of the evaluation should in fact be *part of the process itself*, and merge easily and naturally with on-going activities. In the Freirian sense the methodology will be educational and dialogical, and seek not to impose external interpretations of project outcome, but rather to promote participants' analyses and observations.

3   Critical aspects of the evaluation methodology will be *accessibility* and *scale*. If project participants are to play an active role, then the framework and instruments of the evaluation must not be beyond the capabilities of participants nor of a magnitude to deter their involvement. Massive, complex evaluation exercises, therefore, are out; simple, comprehensible, and easily managed exercises are more appropriate.

4   Another important aspect will be the *timing* of the evaluation. Classically evaluations take place either at a pre-determined break or at the end of project. Such an approach is inappropriate to the evaluation of social development. More appropriately the timing of the evaluation should be linked to the process of social development within the project; it should be a regular and not a one-off exercise. Similarly the timing should relate to the lives of the project participants and not to the demands of external donors.

5   Similarly the issue of *cost* should be considered. In this respect we are talking not only of direct costs attributable to the setting up of the evaluation exercise, but also the indirect costs upon participants' time. The evaluation methodology, therefore, should be sensitive to the demands it might make upon participants' time and should seek to achieve a balance between the need for information and the implications for participants' other responsibilities.

6 Finally any methodology for the evaluation of social development must be *systematic* in nature and follow a regular and agreed course. Social development can be understood only if observations are made systematically and not in a one-off, *ad hoc* fashion. A rhythm of evaluation must be established and preferably internalised within the project, and lead to a continuous and on-going process which is analysed periodically.

In the examples of social development evaluation presented to the workshop, it is impossible to discern any common methodology. Several of the examples were more quantitative in nature and fell within the parameters of conventional project evaluation (McPhail, King and Silkin); others were clearly experimenting with alternative methodologies. Of the others, the works of Brown and Uphoff were more substantial and sought both to outline and detail an appropriate methodology. The essential elements in each of these methodologies is presented here:

1 *Information resources and flows:* Brown argues that the level of democratisation of information flows can serve both as a valid indicator of social development and as a basis for evaluation. An information system, he suggests, provides a more meaningful and less subjective indicator of social development than either normative change or progressive empowerment. Information in this model includes not only the formal information system available to local people, but also a wide range of sources of information which facilitate the survival strategies of those previously excluded from these sources. In using information flows as a key indicator of social development, a number of key questions emerge:

— What are the sources of information available to the target population?
— How does information flow between this population and its environment?
— How does information flow within the population?
— Who controls the information flows?
— How are information flows changing, growing, diminishing or developing?
— What are the relationships between information flows and decision-making?

In comparison to the social development evaluation of what Brown terms 'normative change' or 'progressive empowerment', the evaluation of information resources and flows has several advantages. It is objective, low-cost, people-centred, and essentially a learning model. Empirically the model would be based upon several key indicators:

— the relationship between information flows and decision-making;
— the diversity and range of information flows;
— the permeability and diffusion of information;
— the relationship between the initiation of an information flow and the execution of a related action.

In terms of measurement, Brown suggests three broad areas:

— Measures of *coverage*: volume of information sources and their diversity and range.
— Measures of *direction*: origins of information flows, permeability within the population, and access.
— Measures of *linkage*: networking, exchanges of information, and feedback mechanisms.

Brown's suggested approach to the evaluation of social development, therefore, is based upon the role of information within the social development process. It is at this moment a broad canvas and is as yet untested. However it clearly offers the prospect of anchoring the evaluation into an indicator which can be both quantitative in its aggregation of types of information flow and qualitative in reflecting the magnitude of the social development changes taking place. The key first stage would appear to be to identify and characterise the potential sources and types of information flow and the mechanisms by which these are to be observed within a given population. If information is power, than an assessment of how excluded communities might gain access to relevant information and, equally importantly, how they use it and for what purpose, could usefully indicate and help to 'measure' the social development occurring.

2 *Participatory self-evaluation of project groups*: Uphoff's methodology is derived from work he undertook for the FAO in the latter's People's Participation Programme (PPP) in several countries in Africa. His paper sketches out a field methodology for the participatory self-evaluation of PPP groups and, although the methodology has yet to be systematically tested, it is based upon field work conducted at the project group level. The two key elements in the evaluation methodology are group discussions around a set of questions and the scoring of a group's performance. For example, group members might be asked the question 'Do group members participate in the decision-making process?' The answer involves discussion, which is an indicator of group performance, and also group scoring in response to the question. The whole evaluation exercise, therefore, consists essentially of the systematic formulation of a series of questions, group discussion, and scoring of group performance. As questions are put and discussed, a profile of the group's development should emerge, and the scoring should indicate the extent of the changes which have taken place. Uphoff suggests the following as the steps to be taken in the introduction of this evaluation methodology:

— Reviewing and screening of questions and agreement upon approach relevant to area.
— Drafting of a set of questions.
— Scoring of possible responses to questions.
— Translation of questions into colloquial forms.
— Discussion of approach with project participants.
— Trial run leading to revisions.
— Introduction to groups, presentation of questions, discussion and scoring.
— Revision and analysis.

Uphoff emphasises that project groups cannot be forced to undertake this form of self-evaluation, but they can be encouraged to institutionalise it as an on-going process. Furthermore the methodology is not complete, but should be used to complement other, perhaps more quantitative, techniques. He argues that the exercise is useful, not just for the numbers it might produce, but more importantly for the discussion, which will help to gauge the extent and quality of members' participation in group affairs. The methodology is educational, it helps to distribute responsibility and discover potential leaders, it is simple and does not require complex skills and, most importantly, it is the basis of self-evaluation in which the groups themselves assess progress to date.

Both Brown and Uphoff's proposals attest to the current highly experimental state of the methodology of social development evaluation. Their proposals, as well as those of Altafin, underline the need to move away from the 'numbers game', to identify the qualitative aspects of social development and to ground any evaluation in them. The above examples similarly underline both the *continuous* and *process* nature of qualitative evaluation, and the fact that we should see the evaluation as a series of stages and not as a one-off exercise. The major difficulty we have with these and other proposals, however, is their current lack of empirical support. While we may now be better equipped to conceptualise and structure a

---

Examples of questions and scoring in the evaluation of social development

1 STYLE OF MANAGEMENT: How are group activities managed?

3 = decisions are **always** made with all members' knowledge and participation

2 = decisions are **usually** made with all members' knowledge and participation

1 = decisions are **sometimes** made with all members' knowledge and participation

0 = decisions are **never** made with all members' knowledge and participation

2 INDEPENDENCE FROM GROUP PROMOTER: How able is the group to operate without direction or intervention from the GP?

3 = Group **always** tries to solve a problem itself before taking it up with the GP.

2 = Group **often** tries to solve a problem by itself before seeking the help of the GP.

1 = Group **occasionally** tries to solve a problem by itself.

0 = Group **never** tries to solve a problem by itself.

(Uphoff 1989)

---

social development evaluation exercise, we must still accept its experimental nature and be prepared to innovate and adjust as we go along. Finally the working group concluded its discussion by suggesting the following series of practical steps in the evaluation of social development:

1 Discuss, explore and agree terms of reference or the objectives of the proposed evaluation with all concerned.

2 Clarify the nature of expected outcomes in terms of conclusions or reports. Be prepared to develop more than one type of outcome for different levels.

3 Determine who has responsibility for what: internal and external manpower.

4 Select appropriate methods — check-lists, discussions, data gathering, or group meetings — and be prepared to evolve new ones during the evaluation process.

5   Check out provisional conclusions emerging from the analysis: encourage open debate of them before attempting to put them in final form.
6   Record and report upon the main outcomes of evaluation to all parties involved.

The methodology of social development evaluation: Guayaquil, Ecuador

Guayaquil was chosen as the area to evaluate the social impacts of structural adjustment on low-income households because it was a poor urban community in a country implementing structural adjustment; previous researches were already made in that area, and one of the researchers had some relation with the community's leaders.

The evaluators went to the area with a prepared survey framework. After presenting themselves to the community and explaining what they were doing, two important decisions were taken. First, the contact with the leaders was seen as an important asset to the evaluators, to facilitate their involvement with the community. The choice of these leaders was based on their status, knowledge of the community, and recognition as leaders by the community. Second, the evaluators decided to actually live in the community rather than commuting every day.

Although a previously prepared questionnaire was taken, it was discussed with local leaders, and some supplementary questions were added. The next task was to choose the survey sample. Six blocks already surveyed in 1977 were chosen, and a good description of the houses and a mapping of the sample was undertaken. The sample frame was 461 units, divided into three equal-sized clusters of units (blocks from the early, middle and late 1970s). Then, the evaluators chose three local women with previous community work experience and secondary education to work as remunerated supplementary interviewers. This proved that it was possible to find good field workers from the suburbios themselves.

It took the five interviewers eight days to complete 141 questionnaires (with only a 4 per cent ratio of rejection). (Altogether it took them three weeks from the time they arrived to the end of the first interviews.) They took the results to an outside hotel for four days to analyse the significance of the data collected. They realised that a more detailed understanding was needed on the question of women. Therefore, they decided to undertake another survey in a sub-sample to evaluate the changes in employment patterns and their impact on household structure (i.e. as the income level of men decreased, more women had to work out, and the division of labour within the household was changed — daughters and sons might be doing the mother's work); they also intended to evaluate women's attitudes to fertility, and the implication for children's welfare of the reduction of women's time for reproductive activities. These in-depth follow-up interviews on sensitive issues were undertaken during the long weekend, and it was decided that it would be better to have only women interviewers. Thus along with the female evaluator another woman, who had helped during the first set of interviews, was chosen.

The results of both surveys were discussed with the community during their weekly meetings. Apart from these surveys, a life history methodology was used as complementary to the questionnaire. Secondary data collection through interviews and data collection in health centres, churches, schools and with money lenders and NGOs was also used, as were key informants.

The research experience has proved that a rapid survey in urban areas is possible and that the use of local human resources as social researchers is not only possible but also helps in the understanding of the area and increases the response to the survey. Flexibility and selectivity in choosing researchers and informants should be related to the sensitivity of the questionnaire.

Although the preparation of a research framework in advance is necessary, the evaluator should be prepared to listen to local leaders' opinions and change the direction of the evaluation if it is found necessary. Lastly, the use of long-term contacts is advantageous.

(Sollis and Moser 1989)

Instruments of evaluation

The final and ultimately more detailed dimension of social development evaluation concerns the instruments to be used in the actual evaluation exercise. In this respect it must be said that the papers presented to the working group contained less empirical evidence or suggestions for innovative or imaginative instruments of evaluation. This state of affairs tended to confirm the overall view that the evaluation of social development is still very much at the conceptual and broad framework level, and that we still await substantial evidence of the evaluation in detailed practice. There is no lack of literature on the use of some of the more common, quantitative instruments of evaluation, for example questionnaires, check-lists, secondary sources, and key informants. Such instruments as these certainly do have a role in the evaluation of social development. However, the general contention of the working group was that they were inadequate as the only instruments with which to evaluate social development. Accordingly the group explored a number of alternatives, which can be presented in diagrammatic form (see Table 1).

	Structured	Semi-Structured	Unstructured
O U T S I D E	Survey Questionnaire Content Analysis (Files)	Checklist Interviews	Observations Objective Assessment
I N S I D E	Self- Evaluation Diary	Reciprocal Evaluation	Oral History Reflection Life History

Table 1: Instruments for the evaluation of social development

Table 1 represents the pulling together of several working group discussions and examples in a number of the presented papers. Given the fact that there is no proven list of evaluation instruments, and that social development in its content can range over a broad area, the diagram takes an equally broad span and covers the whole gamut of potential instruments. It distinguishes between *outside* and *inside* instruments and, while it suggests a role for both, it argues at least for balance, if not for greater emphasis upon inside instruments to ensure people's involvement. The instruments in the upper section are already commonly and widely used in evaluation; those in the lower section represent an emerging trend. They range from the more structured and formal exercises of self-evaluation and the keeping of a regular record of activities to the much more open-ended and unstructured use of oral history to assess the change which has taken place. All of this, of course, would be done in the context of the kinds of qualitative indicators which we saw in Section 2. Furthermore the working group suggested a series of aids which would assist the use of the above instruments.

Prompts	*Recording*
Questionnaires	Writing notes
Check-lists	Audio recording
Pictures	Video recording
Project schedules	Diagrams
	Graphical presentations

The issue of evaluation instruments is, of course, substantial in its own right, and there is still much to be done both to document and to refine some of the 'inside' instruments. These latter instruments will be more closely related to the qualitative indicators of social development, and clearly present problems of *recording, information storage,* and *interpretation.* The working group did not touch upon these aspects, but suggested that considerable work still needed to be done. Any experience to date on the use and interpretation of qualitative indicators of social development is scattered in the practice of hundreds of projects, and no systematic review has ever been undertaken. In summary the methodological steps would appear to be:

1 Identification of the instruments to be used to monitor predetermined indicators, with emphasis upon a balance between structured and unstructured means.
2 The choice of appropriate aids to facilitate the collection of data, information, and observations around the indicators.
3 A system whereby these data, information and observations could be stored and retrieved when necessary at appropriate stages in the evaluation process.
4 The interpretation of the data, information, and observations, using a variety of diagrammatic and other forms of presentation.

Points (3) and (4) were not considered in any depth by the working group, which indeed reflects the lack of substantial material to date on these issues, and points the way to a future research agenda for donor agencies interested in improving their evaluation of social development.

Instruments used in social development evaluation: Guayaquil, Ecuador

— use of long-term contact available (NGOs, churches, etc.);
— development of a relationship with local leaders;
— use of a previous framework questionnaire but open-ended for any supplementary information;
— consultation with leaders about the questionnaire content;
— flexibility on changing the objective of the research;
— selection of surveyed area based on systematic techniques;
— use of local people as interviewers;
— remunerated interviewers;
— living in the community when possible to have easier access to information;
— use of second survey in a sub-sample to deepen understanding;
— life-history methodology as complementary to questionnaire of sub-sample;
— secondary data collection;
— interviews with school teachers, health officer, church leaders and money lenders.

(Sollis and Moser, 1989)

Concluding comments

It was suggested in the working group that the methodology of evaluation of social development required '... an entire shift of perspective'. If this is true, then it must be recognised that this 'entire shift' is still taking place and is not yet concluded. The papers presented on methodology confirmed that this shift of perspective is underway, but that it is still largely exploratory. The papers were strong on conceptualisation and on a broad framework for evaluation methodology, but more tentative on the practical aspects of instruments, aids, and information storage and retrieval. The papers of Sollis and Moser, Uphoff and McPhail were more substantial in this respect, although the latter was largely quantitative in orientation. Collectively, however, the papers emphasised that any methodology of evaluation must place project participants centre stage; such an approach increased the likelihood that data and information collected would not only be appropriate but would remain local and ensure that locally owned means of collection were used. In this way the methodology would be developmental and not merely an instrument of outsider control. In order to achieve this 'people's emphasis', it was suggested that the methodology employed should as far as possible be based on unstructured observations, rather than structured surveys, and should place more weight on the subjective views of 'insiders', than on the objective views of 'outsiders'.

To help ensure that proposed methods and instruments are people-conscious and not entirely outside-oriented, Taylor's series of questions can also serve as a useful framework:

— For whom are we doing the evaluation ?
— What do we want to evaluate ?
— When are we going to evaluate ?
— Who is going to undertake or play a part in the evaluation ?
— How are we going to evaluate the project's outcomes ?

Eventually the whole exercise has to be reduced to and included in some kind of report. The report is a vital part of the evaluation methodology, since its contents serve as the basic material for continuing evaluation. There is little scientific basis to evaluation reports; but their structure and content needs careful thought if they are to help in the understanding of the process. The first step in the evaluation methodology is the agreement between insiders and outsiders of the indicators to be evaluated; the last step is the documentation which contains the evaluation's results agreed by all actors. Only a carefully thought-out methodology can offer the prospect of a successful progression from the first to the last step.

Papers submitted to the working group on the methodology of social development evaluation

Iara Altafin: 'Participatory Communication in Social Development Evaluation'

David Brown: 'Methodological Considerations in the Evaluation of Social Development Programmes: An Alternative Approach'

Stephen King and Trish Silkin: 'CAFOD-ERA Evaluation Case study: Eritrea, The Mogoraib-Forto Regional Comprehensive Development Programme'

Kathryn McPhail: 'Impact Evaluation of World Bank Agriculture and Rural Development Projects: Methodology and Selected Findings'

Peter Sollis and Caroline Moser: 'A Methodological Framework for Analysing the Social Costs of Adjustment: Guayaquil, Ecuador'

Laurence Taylor: 'Participatory Evaluation with NGOs: Some Experiences of Informal and Exploratory Methodologies'

Norman Uphoff: 'A Field Methodology for Participatory Self-Evaluation of PPP Group and Inter-group Association Performance'

Laura Vargas: 'Reflections on the Methodology of Evaluation'

SECTION 4

PARTNERSHIP IN SOCIAL
DEVELOPMENT EVALUATION

4.1 Partnership in social development evaluation: Thematic paper

Rajesh Tandon

Introduction

The question of partnership in social development evaluation cannot be raised and discussed without specific reference to the meaning of social development and social development evaluation. I will reiterate my own understanding of social development evaluation, in order to create the context for my comments about partnership and social development evaluation.

For me, social development evaluation is an intervention in the ongoing efforts of promoting developmental initiatives. In our experience, this intervention needs to have several characteristics if it is to promote authentic and genuine processes and initiatives of social development in a given context. Some of these characteristics are listed below.

1 Social development evaluation has to be seen as *an educational intervention* in the ongoing process of development. Its educational nature is focusing on the learning of those who are involved in promoting, catalysing, and sustaining such development initiatives. In our context this implies that evaluation must be seen and experienced as a learning opportunity for all those constituencies which are involved in a specific development context. These constituencies may comprise the poor and the oppressed, as well as those who are animating and promoting the development of the poor and the oppressed. The specific composition of the constituencies will vary from situation to situation. But it is important that evaluation becomes an educational experience for these relevant constituencies.

2 Social development evaluation has to be seen as *an intervention which in itself becomes developmental* for the processes and initiatives being undertaken on the ground. If an intervention is developmental in nature, rather than judgemental, it can then be utilised to further inspire, energise and revitalise development initiatives and take them to the next level of growth and maturity.

3 Social development evaluation has to be seen as an intervention which enhances the sense of confidence and the capacity among key constituencies involved in any development initiative. Thus this intervention in itself must be *an empowering intervention*, as opposed to a belittling or undermining one. As a consequence of social developmental evaluation, key constituencies engaged in a developmental initiative must feel a greater sense of purpose, commitment to that purpose, and enhanced faith in their capacities to accomplish that purpose.

4 And finally, social development evaluation must be seen as *an intervention that attempts to clarify objectives and future strategies* either through restatement or reformulation. Thus social development evaluation is not limited to an explanation of the historical events of what happened, but also needs to help clarify where we are heading. Recognising the dynamic and continuous nature of any social development effort, the evaluation must attempt to link an understanding of the past with a vision of the future. If it does not create that possibility, it becomes a static intervention which may explain very clearly what happened and why, but does not help to clarify the future directions and strategies for that initiative.

The meaning of partnership

What is the meaning of partnership in social development evaluation, if the evaluation we are talking about has such characteristics as those listed above? What is the purpose of partnership in social development evaluation?

It appears to me that the foregoing characteristics of an effective social development evaluation become the very rationale for ensuring effective partnership in such an evaluation process. Therefore, the partnership is not merely an instrumental concept, which helps us accomplish some results which we would otherwise not have been able to achieve; partnership in social development evaluation is fundamentally linked to our philosophy of development. If our philosophy of development puts people at the centre, if we believe that development cannot be done from outside but can only be sustained and elaborated by a group of people on their own (perhaps with external support), and if we believe that development is not merely a series of events but a combination of qualitative processes, organisations, and people spread over a period of time, then we have to see that *partnership* is fundamental to any such social·development effort.

Partnership is essential between multiple constituencies and within constituencies. Given a particular group of poor people in a society that is generally poor, social development may require building partnerships across sub-units and clusters of the poor. Partnership may also entail helping to build linkages and supportive mechanisms between constituencies of the poor and those who are animating, catalysing, or promoting development initiatives with these constituencies. This is where the role of field workers, activists, organisers, and other voluntary organisations becomes relevant. Partnership may also entail linkages with other constituencies, like those of the donors, at the local, regional, national or international levels. Partnership may entail linkages with like-minded constituencies, people's organisations, and voluntary agencies. Partnership may entail a variety of other linkages which help to contribute to the strengthening of the processes of development being initiated and sustained by the poor. Therefore, partnership is a fundamental concept in the very idea of social development as we envisage it, and any sustainable, long-term, and self-reliant development requires building and maintaining strong partnerships across like-minded constituencies. Therefore, the question of partnership in social development evaluation is preceded by the question of partnership in social development itself.

It is our experience that partnership in social development evaluation cannot function if the very processes and mechanisms of the social development initiatives do not incorporate, and believe in, partnership *per se*. It is only when partnership is seen as a fundamental tenet of social development that it can be brought into focus in evaluation. This, therefore, becomes a major constraint in trying to think about partnership and social development evaluation. Our experience suggests that where such partnerships have not been encouraged, promoted, and sustained within the development initiatives, it is impossible to promote or implement ideas of partnership in evaluation of those development efforts.

The second point in relation to partnership and social development evaluation relates to the nature of partnerships and the manner in which they are initiated, sustained and matured. Our experience suggests that partnership between unequal partners is very hard to build and maintain. Where a particular constituency feels relatively powerless and incapable in relation to another constituency, it is very difficult to build the bridges of partnership between them. Thus a notion of mutuality and of give-and-take, and a recognition that I can contribute something and that you also can contribute something, are all essential prerequisites for building any partnership across such constituencies. This has implications for partnership in social development evaluation as well. In the process of devising an evaluation, the question of partnership is determined by the nature of the constituencies and their perceptions about each other. Where the constituency of the poor and the oppressed does not feel a sense of mutuality and shared vision with the constituency of the animators, organisers, or voluntary agencies, building partnership becomes a problematic exercise. Therefore, partnership in evaluation between these two constituencies in a developmental context can be built, sustained, and utilised only if there are shared perceptions and an equitable relationship.

It is in this context that our experiences have shown the difficulty, in the course of a given social development evaluation, of building partnership with donors, particularly those who operate at the international level. Most constituencies of the poor and those of voluntary organisations or animators tend to perceive donors as all-powerful and, therefore, experience unequal starting points in their relationship. It is in such situations that attempts to build partnership in social development evaluation between a grassroots organisation and its international donor have not succeeded. Our experiences have shown that it is better to recognise the difficulties in this explicitly and to create conditions for mutual dialogue and debate somewhere in the process of evaluation, than to overlook or ignore fundamental differences between constituencies and the obstacles to building and sustaining partnerships between them.

The other important aspect in the question of partnership is the quality of relationship that is built between members of the constituencies. Partnership is not merely an intellectual camaraderie or convergence of ideas and frameworks. On the contrary, partnership is a human dimension; it is a relationship between individuals and groups of people which goes beyond the mind and the intellect, and enters the heart and the emotions. Therefore, partnership requires a sharing of visions, dreams, hopes, fears, aspirations, and frustrations among members of the project constituencies. Partnerships, therefore, take a long time to be built, and require careful nurturing in order to be sustained. To attempt a sudden, short-duration, quick-fix partnership during a limited-purpose social development evaluation exercise will be both unrealistic and difficult. In fact, our experience suggests that partnership in social development evaluation is possible only when there has been some history of sharing and understanding across constituencies.

So there is a related aspect to the question of partnership which in operational terms has a great deal of relevance. It has to do with the nature, both in terms of depth and quality, of partnership. All partnerships between different constituencies in development contexts are not necessarily of the same depth and quality. It is possible to conceptualise and operationalise different degrees of partnership across different constituencies in a given social development evaluation exercise. The specific context of a social development initiative will help us identify the depth and quality of partnership that can be built and sustained during an evaluation exercise. Therefore, to expect uniformly similar quality and depth of partnership in all social development evaluation exercises across all constituencies is unrealistic.

Finally, there is the question of intervention to bring about and sustain partnerships in social development evaluation. This is where the role of facilitation is crucial and relevant. In our experience we have found that the most important function that we can perform in a social development evaluation exercise is to facilitate mutual understanding, reflection, and learning across constituencies involved in the social development. So our fundamental role has been to facilitate the building and learning from partnerships across constituencies in any given evaluation exercise. The facilitation of social development evaluation may, therefore, require the ability to relate to diverse constituencies simultaneously, and to be able to create mechanisms for dialogue, reflection and learning in a framework of equality and shared vision across these different constituencies.

In this respect the question of tools and techniques becomes relevant, since it is within the fundamental framework of partnership that the question of methods and techniques of data-collection, analysis, and reflection becomes important. It is here that we can utilise both quantitative and qualitative ways of collecting information, and analysing and making sense of data.

This is important because some constituencies may feel more comfortable in using stories, drawings, songs, role-plays, theatre, puppetry, and similar other forms of data collection and analysis, while others may feel more familiar and comfortable with questionnaires, in-depth interviews, surveys and the like. It is not, however, a question of one method being better than the other. What is important is the judicious selection and utilisation of methods which respond to the diversity of constituencies in the context of building partnerships across them to facilitate the reflection of, and learning from, a given social development initiative. Therefore, the question of methods of data collection and analysis, the question of tools and techniques of evaluation cannot be answered without this essential framework of partnership in social development evaluation.

The fundamental question in any social development evaluation is *whose interest does the evaluation serve?* Who benefits from the evaluation? Do the constituencies of the poor and the oppressed benefit from the evaluation? Do these constituencies control and regulate the evaluation process, and do they utilise the results of the evaluation in their own interests? Or does the evaluation become the requirement of the donors and those who define the broad framework of policies under which the specific social development initiative is undertaken? Is the evaluation then subtly, and even at times overtly, controlled and regulated by those who provide resources and policy support for grassroots development initiatives? Does the evaluation become an exercise in which the pet theories and favourite hobby-horses of the resource providers and policy-makers get reaffirmed and pushed?

These are the central questions in any social development evaluation exercise. They are related to our fundamental philosophy of social development, our view of the world, our view of social change processes. What is the role of development: are people in the centre, or are they on the periphery? Our responses to these central questions are crucial in any serious discussion of partnership and the tools and techniques of social development evaluation. Without this essential clarity, partnership in social development evaluation becomes merely technocratic and instrumental, as opposed to philosophical and critical.

4.2 Partnership in social development evaluation: Review of workshop papers and discussion

Introduction

In trying to find better ways to evaluate the more qualitative aspects of social development projects and programmes, this working group considered the role of partnership in the evaluation process. It examined the value of less rigid and more flexible and responsive approaches to evaluation. A list of papers presented for discussion by this working group is to be found at the end of this section.

In his introductory paper, 'Partnership in Social Development Evaluation', Rajesh Tandon argued that, to be genuine, an evaluation had to be educational for all social groups involved. This was necessary in order to enhance the programme or project being evaluated, as well as to give a sense of purpose and involvement to all engaged in the work. In addition to being retrospective, the evaluation must be forward-looking through a consideration of the aims and vision of the project. To enable this to happen, a partnership which brings together the different actors in the project community must be established.

Tandon asserted that partnership is essential for social development, to *empower the poor to initiate their own development* through the development of linkages between similar organised groups. Such a partnership is not easy to build. The relationship between the poor, local non-government agencies, and international donors is, in terms of their respective powers, an unequal one. It will take considerable time to build up relationships of trust and mutual understanding. Building such trust is part of the purpose of the evaluation which aims at creating mechanisms for dialogue and reflection.

There must also be a wide range of evaluation tools available to evaluators to facilitate this process and to enable them to tailor their evaluations to particular cases. There can be no universal rules for such a process. This flexible approach may draw on less formal qualitative information, such as that derived from drawings and songs, as well as quantitative surveys and interviews. The evaluators must share in the visions and hopes of the participants, and gear the evaluation to the benefit of the people rather than to that of the resource providers. To ensure success, the partnership must be flexible enough to include all the parties involved. The key themes of Tandon's introductory paper are the need for *learning*, the need for *dialogue, contact,* and *communication*, and thus for qualitative forms of evaluation.

Political and cultural influences on evaluation

Koenraad Verhagen's paper, 'Evaluation in Partnership: Attractive Utopia or Deceptive Illusion?', considered the conceptual, political and cultural dimensions of evaluation, and their influence on partnership as a part of the evaluation process. He underlined his argument by maintaining that self-evaluation is at the root of all human progress, and must be incorporated into a renegotiated evaluation process. Social development evaluation involves a number of parties, such as:

— The 'social actors', people at the grass roots, mostly grouped into formal or informal People's Organisations or 'membership organisations'.
— The 'agents' of development carrying out catalytic and support functions, (semi-) professional staff, and employed by a local non-governmental development organisation.
— The 'funders', staff employed by funding agency.

All three parties should participate in the evaluation process, as subjects. They can engage outsiders or ask for outside help in the process of self-evaluation. This engagement of outsiders is current practice in most evaluations.

Verhagen also provides us with definitions of different sorts of evaluations that enhance partnership between groups who are members of the project community:

a. *Self-evaluation* implies that the subject and object of evaluation merge into one entity. During or at the end of the process the evaluating party pronounces a judgement on its own performance.
b. A *joint evaluation* is one where two parties carry out jointly an evaluation. It may or may not constitute a self-evaluation.
c. The term *participatory evaluation* is often used to denote substantial participation by the social actors, and when it focuses on those social actors it is very similar to self-evaluation.
d. *Mutual evaluation* occurs when two parties evaluate each other's performance.

Some believe that evaluation should be objective and neutral, and thus argue that the participative approach, by its very nature, cannot facilitate this. Conversely there are those who argue that the objective and external types of evaluation are in conflict with the principles of partnership, equality, and reciprocity. Verhagen maintains that a balance between external and internal elements is optimally required. In analysing the political dimensions of evaluations, this issue of objectivity and value neutrality is central. There are those who argue for more precise assessments of efficiency and impact in order to satisfy the demands for accountability in the disbursement of public funds. The demands for managerial control over expenditure are supposedly met through impartial analysis and objective study. Such studies, Verhagen argues, flagrantly contradict the proclaimed ideals of partnership, equality, and reciprocity. New evaluation paradigms are advocated and increasingly practised within the NGO system. These new forms of evaluation are not formal substitutes for external evaluations. They may in fact be more intrusive if all they do is further the control that the evaluator is able to exert over that which is evaluated. Self-evaluation is a means of appraisal whereby the organisation is able to assess its own activities and change direction if necessary.

Statements about joint evaluation

When two parties, each under its own responsibility, undertake an evaluation and have decided to collaborate in one or more stages of the evaluation with a view to coming to a common judgement about the evaluandum (which should, of course, be partly or entirely the same), we can call it a joint evaluation. One can imagine different forms of joint evaluation. The statements below refer to a situation where a funding agency, responsible for the composition of the external evaluation team, and a local non-governmental development organisation (NGDO) or people's organisation (PO), engaged in self-evaluation, have decided to join their efforts for such a purpose.

1 External evaluation in principle can be a useful complement to self-evaluation. For fruitful interaction between evaluators from both sides, a certain number of conditions must be met concerning attitudes, expectations, and timing and organisation, such as further specified in the following paragraphs.

2 The external evaluation should not take place when the programme/ project period is nearing its end. It should take place rather at the beginning when financial support for the years to come is already

---

ensured. This goes against the logic of project financing, but fits well into the logic of long-term organisation-centred support and partnership.

3   Terms of reference determining objectives, scope, and organisation of the self-evaluation and the external evaluation cannot and should not be similar. But differences in orientation and the distinct responsibilities of each of the parties involved should be discussed, with their implications for timing and organisation of field trips, exchange of findings, consultations, and reporting. Self and external evaluators may have different perceptions and expectations of each other's roles.

4   External evaluators, in order to be able to assess the position of the NGDO/POs in their societal context and with a view to diversifying their sources of information, may wish to contact other organisations — non-governmental or governmental — and seek opinions from them rather than being restricted to the NGDO/POs (the evaluandum) as the only source of information. This may considerably annoy the NGDO/PO concerned and affect the spirit of partnership during the joint evaluation.

5   The questioning by external evaluators (foreign or local) of an organisation's ideology (system of values) is a sensitive issue. Does one have the right to do this? Equally sensitive is discussion of perceived inconsistencies between ideology and practice.

6   External evaluations can be especially helpful in the interpretation of self-evaluation findings and their possible implications for funding agency/NGDO or PO relationship.

7   Joint evaluation can sometimes be more effective where it takes place in an informal manner than where it has been deliberately organised.

8   Since virtually all evaluations take place in the Third World, there is a tendency to under-analyse the effect of the policies and administrative practices of funding agencies on the performance of the organisations they finance. Funding agencies tend to remain out of scope as objects of evaluation.

9   Evaluation in partnership does not imply that the different parties involved should come to the same conclusions. Perfect unanimity would rather be indicative of superficiality of the evaluation and of an immature relationship (or of a combination of both), than of good partnership.

(Verhagen 1989)

A desire for a restructured evaluation is accompanied by changing power relations within the NGO aid system itself. As Verhagen points out:

> 'Recipient' organisations, especially the larger ones with an international reputation, are operating more and more in a buyer's market. Their 'bargaining position' has strengthened with the multiplication and diversification of multilateral and bilateral donor agencies seeking more meaningful outlets for their funding in the NGO sector ... In this way the 'market forces' prevailing in the aid system also facilitate the development of more equality and reciprocity in funder/agent relationships.
> (Verhagen 1989)

Non-government organisations today are not so tied to the limited sources of funding that were available previously. They can thus afford to be selective in their choice of methodologies for evaluation, encouraging partnership and self-evaluation wherever possible. But the aid system will always have the power to inhibit the development partnership. Too much money chasing too few good projects puts NGOs of the South in a potentially powerful position.

Verhagen concluded his paper by suggesting that the fundamental question in evaluation of social development programmes is *who should evaluate the activities of whom?* In addition to the external/internal dichotomy, there is the understanding that all evaluations serve the political interests of different people/organisations in different ways. The rationale for bringing in external evaluators depends on the objectivity and impartiality which they should be able to contribute.

Cultural bias is unavoidable

Cultural bias of one sort or another is an additional problem in the development of partnership. Evaluators may have different perceptions of religion, poverty, equality, and income and employment generation from the people being evaluated. Project documents usually make distinctions between the secular and the religious or sacred spheres of life. Funding agencies tend to operate in primarily secular terms, whereas for the villagers a much more holistic perspective may make the separation between secular and religious impossible. Similarly, while funders are interested in combatting poverty expressed in terms of material deprivation, so-called beneficiaries might be much more concerned with poverty which they see in terms of moral and personal deprivation — degrading conditions which diminish their status and self-esteem. Income and employment generation may not be so important as looking for opportunities to save time and money, through preventing losses, rather than earning wages through paid employment which may be regarded as degrading. Villagers may not perceive projects in terms of the achievement of project objectives, nor will they necessarily be so politically motivated as those who argue for their empowerment. They may judge projects in terms of the increased unity that they have brought to the community, rather than in terms of increased productivity.

It is important to admit that actors, agents, and funders operate in and retain an attachment to different cultures. Performance is likely to be judged on the bases of different value systems. This can be partly circumvented if the evaluator is aware of other modes of explanation and alternative conceptions. The process of finding different answers and solutions from a range of different sources may strengthen an evaluation.

The need for discussion and dialogue between those involved in the evaluation of a project is a theme which carries over into the notes made by John MacDonald. In these notes — 'Who speaks for the people in participatory evaluations?' — MacDonald illustrates the way in which participation and discussion form the basis of the evaluation. Evaluators must 'dialogue with the responses' to such qualitative questions as 'What have you achieved in this programme?' which are asked at village-level meetings. In this way the community evaluates what has happened and influences future decisions. But the question of the representativity of those who 'speak for the people' remains problematic. Intermediaries between outsiders and insiders tend to be marginal to both cultures, and thus not necessarily the best people to trust for interpretations.

The concept of partnership associated with sharing and the development of common concerns is dealt with in Pramod Unia's paper, entitled 'Social Action Group Strategies for Oxfam in the Indian Sub-continent'. The positive aspects of partnership are stressed in a discussion of social action groups. These were formed during the 1970s as a way of mobilising and empowering the poor in the pursuit of common interests. Emphasis is laid on the need for shared beliefs between groups, and common goals in order to make the partnership work.

These social action groups have become viable and important alternatives in implementing people-oriented development programmes. The assessment of the groups' own social development is achieved through a focus on educational needs, an understanding of basic rights related to land issues, wages, and environmental concerns. Partnership is founded on an understanding that social change can be brought about only through social and political mobilisation of and by the poor.

Self-evaluation

Philippe Egger's paper, 'Village Groups Evaluate Their Activities: An Experience in Mali', provides an illustration of the work of the International Labour Organisation's Programme on Participatory Organisations of the Rural Poor, and documents an experience of self-evaluation carried out by organised village groups in three areas of Mali. The NGO responsible is called Six S (an acronym for 'Se Servir de la Saison Seche en Savane et au Sahel'). Six S helps organised groups through a flexible fund providing both grants and credit on the basis of matching funds raised from groups. Locally available ideas, energy, and resources are pooled, and traditional mutual help practices are transformed into organised forward-looking development initiatives. Six S stresses the importance of self-evaluation, which it sees as consisting of five phases:

a. Initial orientation and training session: 8 days, 15 participants from base groups + facilitator.
b. Self-evaluation exercise: 3-4 days per month over 3 months involving base group assemblies.
c. Review of first results: 10 days involving same group as in phase 1.
d. Analysis and report preparation: 3 months, involving a facilitator and Six S staff.
e. Reporting of results: 8 days, involving base groups and facilitator.

Stages (a), (b) and (c) had been completed by September 1989, and some preliminary results were available. During the initial orientation stage, six basic evaluation tools were elaborated. Each tool is composed of a series of key questions. These tools are described in the accompanying box. It is too early to draw anything but tentative conclusions about the effectiveness of these evaluation tools, and it is certain that they will need to be adapted in some ways in the future.

Egger, like Tandon and Unia, argued that group analysis of group activities is fundamental, both within and between groups. It must avoid apportioning blame for failures. Participants have to learn how to 'speak up' and achieve a gradual agreement with others. Egger further sees self-evaluation as a *subjective learning process* which encourages people to become aware of themselves, and to take responsibility for their future social development. This in turn will promote self-reliance and the ability to reflect critically on past and present achievements. This is something which echoes Tandon's understanding that evaluations must include a vision and strategy for the future, as well as assessing historical developments.

Evaluation tools for self-evaluation, Six S, Mali

EVALUATION TOOLS QUESTIONS

1 Activity evaluation	— What is the history of the activity? — What are the signs of good and bad health of the activity? — What are the results of the activity? — Who benefits/doesn't benefit from the activity? — Who does what for the success/failure of the activity? — Unresolved problems and suggestions
2 Survey of activities in the zone	Activities/Quantities — last 3 dry seasons
3 Results	What results for a better life?
4 Financial survey of the zone	Table on incomes (Six S funds, savings, other incomes, loan repayments) and expenditures — last 3 dry seasons.
5 Animation work in the zone	— History of animation work — What are the signs of good and bad health in animation work? — What results for more dynamic groups?

(Egger 1989)

The themes of *discussion, communication* and *increasing self-awareness* in the process of self-evaluation are emphasised in Marie-Therese Feuerstein's paper — 'Partnership in Social Development Evaluation'. Her study of a Bihari Community Health Department looked at a self-evaluation which began with a six-day training programme for the evaluators, to introduce them to a variety of evaluative tools — both qualitative and quantitative approaches, staff and village meetings, questionnaires, and analyses of patient records. What emerged from the participatory evaluation was much useful information which highlighted areas of neglect within the community. One evaluator commented that 'during the survey I saw the real condition of the women'. The findings of the self-evaluation will be used to educate, train and mobilise people at community level, and to plan future social development projects.

Finally, Bandyopadhyay's paper on problems of self-sustained agriculture stressed the need to understand farmers' perspectives — the opportunities and constraints that they themselves feel, and the rationalities that lie behind certain sorts of decision-making procedures.

Only beginning from what a farmer considers useful and worthwhile to sustain, from the level of his [sic] consciousness and his appreciation of his own reality, we may expect to be successful in persuading him to gain confidence and bridge gaps which are thwarting his capabilities to move ahead.
(Bandyopadhyay 1989)

Conflicts of interest

On the negative side, partnership in social development evaluation is not easy to achieve. The conflict of interests and the unequal power of the groups involved can make dialogue and agreement difficult. The political and cultural dichotomies which may exist between the evaluator and the evaluated can take a long time to disappear. Verhagen stressed the need for dialogue and broad-mindedness in these situations, and the need to acknowledge differences. There is a constant danger of the evolution of anti-participatory conditions, enshrined in hierarchical structures, and of fragmentation, and thus a constant danger of losing sight of original objectives. To avoid this, the development of appropriate communication and information networks is vital. This can ensure that perspectives are broadened and wider issues are explored, as groups are linked to like-minded groups. There is a limit to what individual groups can achieve, but links with others strengthen collective purposes.

When trying to build up partnership we must take into account regional and national differences which offer different opportunities and constraints. In some circumstances it is going to be difficult to build up partnerships in the ways in which one might desire. Partnership can be attained only when beneficiaries start perceiving the importance of evaluation and begin the process themselves. People at different levels in the project community have different perspectives, but partnership can be built up through focusing on the twin processes of monitoring and evaluation. The monitoring process helps to broaden access to information, and can be an empowering act in itself. It also makes evaluations more productive by overcoming the problems of time which traditionally hinder evaluations. The process of continuous monitoring and evaluation negates the need for a rushed job at the end. Monitoring should happen at all levels simultaneously; it is not just the monitoring of the implementation process as it affects the beneficiaries. It should also be seen not as an alternative to evaluation, but rather as a complement.

Finally, a series of related issues which emerged from the working groups' discussions included:

1 *Evaluator as facilitator:* Similarly, evaluation should take place at all levels simultaneously. These levels come together in terms of the evaluator who is able to articulate the different interests represented in the project community, and is thus able to make explicit those areas of work which are problematic and which resist the development of a philosophy of partnership. In this sense it might be more useful to see the evaluator as more of a facilitator, bringing together different processes and exercises in order to break down internal prejudices and assumptions. It is necessary for all constituents within the project to be able to step outside the day-to-day routine and to see their work from another angle. In large-scale organisations the role of the internal auditor, someone who is able to do this, has expanded rapidly in recent years, and it might be worthwhile learning from the skills that have been developed in this area, and translating them into the requirements of the project community in the field of social development.

2 *Indigenous evaluations:* Indigenous evaluations which give reasons why people do or do not participate in social development projects and programmes need to be recovered and incorporated into re-designed evaluation methodologies, so that they are truly participatory. They can then reflect the indigenous values that people themselves use and can be important indicators of effectiveness and viability which are often lost to outsiders. But what are the most effective methods of recovering this information?

3 *Knowledge and awareness:* There is a crucial link between knowledge and social awareness, and one of the indicators of success in building partnership is the level of awareness that people reach. One indicator of whether groups have reached this point is whether or not they are capable of coping with the perceived unpleasant aspects of evaluation. They learn from mistakes and build stronger capacity, moving from what has been termed a 'naive consciousness' where personal blame is attached to failure, to a more 'critical consciousness' where collective responsibility for failure is accepted, or where there is a recognition of the complexities associated with attaching blame, and an understanding of the constraints presented by the wider socio-political environment in which they are living. Once this point is reached, there is a recognition that evaluation is a two-way process and also that the relationship between donors and beneficiaries is more than merely a question of financial flows in one direction. The importance of educating a wider public in the North becomes central to the building of partnership, so that cultural distances might be decreased and the ethnocentric myths that inhibit understanding about the nature of relationships between North and South might be countered.

4 *Encouraging partnership:* In order to encourage the development of partnership there are several areas that need to be given greater attention. There needs to be more work done on the tools that might be used for self-evaluation, and on the elaboration of ways in which the views of beneficiary groups and organisations might be more easily and effectively heard. How might communication between different partners and different levels within the project community be improved? How can one develop external support for self-evaluation, and how can indigenous capacities be re-asserted? Is one of the ways to train people indigenously? What can that mean?

Papers submitted to the working group on partnership in social development evaluation

Suraj Bandyopadhyay: 'Problems of Self-Sustained Agriculture: Observations on Rain-fed Farming in Eastern India'

Philippe Egger: 'Village Groups Evaluate Their Activities: An Experience in Mali'

Marie Therese Feuerstein: 'Participatory Evaluation in Patna — A Case Study from Bihar, India, of a Health and Social Development Programme'

John MacDonald: 'Who Speaks "For the People" in Participatory Evaluations?'

Pramod Unia: 'Social Action Group Strategies for Oxfam in the Indian Sub-Continent'

Koenraad Verhagen: 'Evaluation in Partnership: Attractive Utopia or Deceptive Illusion?'

SECTION 5

THE EVALUATOR IN SOCIAL DEVELOPMENT EVALUATION

5.1 The evaluator in social development evaluation: Thematic paper

Delle Tiongson-Brouwers

Introduction

A friend once told me that she has two descriptions of an evaluator. The first: an evaluator is like an accountant who tells you that you have no more money and it is too late for you to do anything about it. The second: an evaluator is one who confuses you with many recommendations because he himself (or she herself) is confused.

To evaluate is to assess. One can assess an activity after it is over; or one can evaluate the plan prior to its execution. For example, a football coach can evaluate how the game went; or he can assess his game plan even before the game starts. In social development, the former is generally known as project evaluation, the latter as proposal evaluation. In project evaluation the focus is on what has been accomplished *vis à vis* stipulated objectives. For proposal evaluation, the relevance of objectives and strategies in relation to the particular milieu and problems is a key area of inquiry.

In both proposal and project assessment, the evaluator has to deal with two basic clients: the development funding agency (DFA) and the proponent or project holder. Both have pragmatic needs and concerns: the DFA has the need to channel resources to the right project; and the proponent has the wish to get his or her project funded. Thus, the evaluator is like a tight-rope-walker, whose credibility rests on maintaining a scrupulous balance.

Project proposals are indispensable for getting funds. When a proponent sends a proposal to a DFA, the request is studied, for example, according to its content and clarity of presentation. It has been common practice for DFAs to make decisions based solely on the information contained in the proposal. This was not because the DFAs found it the most efficient process, but because of the absence of or unfamiliarity with alternative methods. In some cases decisions were made by people who had never been to the country where the project originated. I remember meeting years ago an Asian Desk Officer of a DFA. This particular Desk Officer for

Asia had never set foot on Asian soil! It is very encouraging that this could probably not now happen.

In the Philippines, the evaluation of proposals for social development projects can be traced back to the early 1970s as a concrete response to the expressed need of DFAs. Being thousands of kilometres away from the project environment, DFAs began searching for ways by which they could be properly advised about the urgency and relevance of a project that was requesting assistance. The DFAs sought advice from local partners who were considered knowledgeable about the situation of the intended project beneficiaries.

One of my vivid memories in this work was when I evaluated a proposal for a project in a far-flung rural area. Without leaving my desk, and without going out of our air-conditioned office in Manila, I wrote a four-page assessment of the proposal in a relatively short time. As a novice, I thought this was a great accomplishment. 'What you have done is an armchair evaluation,' my friend remarked. 'You are like the author,' she continued, 'who dared to write the history of Europe just because he flew over the continent.' Fortunately, armchair evaluations are things of the past. Today emphasis is given to a process that is more participative and people-oriented. Now there is a clearer realisation that an evaluation is done not because it is a requirement of the DFA, but because projects which can contribute to social change deserve to be assisted and funded. From being mainly a service to DFAs, evaluation has evolved into a means for training people's organisations and other types of proponents in improving the technical feasibility and social relevance of their projects.

The role of evaluators

Evaluators play various roles in relation to the different components and aspects of project and/or proposal evaluation. These components can be categorised into DFAs, proponent or project holder, the project itself and the community where the project originates.

In relation to *development funding agencies*, the evaluator is a source of information. The information which the evaluator provides becomes an input for the DFA's decision-making on the proposal and, on a more long-term basis, may influence the priorities of the DFA for a given country. A responsible adviser should express and communicate the interest and needs of the target beneficiaries, and facilitate the DFA's understanding of how a project responds to a specific need within a given milieu.

A corresponding responsibility that DFAs need to address is the issue of confidentiality. A local evaluator may request DFAs to keep his or her evaluations confidential because of the sensitive content of the assessment.

DFAs, on the other hand, might find it convenient to quote the local evaluator and openly ascribe to him or her the observations on a project, instead of making the comments as their own.

A third-party evaluation should be considered as merely advisory in nature. The evaluator does not make the decision whether the proposal should be funded or not. DFAs are the ones who make the final decision, hence they should take the advice as their own if they believe in it, or completely disregard the evaluator's opinion if they find it not to be factual and not to coincide with their own assessment of the project.

In relation to the *project holder*, the evaluator takes on the role of a friendly adviser. More often, proponents view the evaluator as an outsider, an unwelcome and unavoidable intruder whose assessment can either open or close the funding taps for the project. This is because evaluations often contain recommendations to DFAs. Consequently the evaluator is seen as someone who has the power to sway the decision of the DFA. Given such a perception, the evaluator needs to show understanding for the project holder's apprehensions.

It is important for the evaluator to get the message across to the proponents that the existence of the evaluation exercise does not confer on him or her the power of decision regarding the project. The proponent has the power to decide the *what* and *how* of a project; the DFA decides how much to fund. This power structure remains basically unchanged, even with the entry of the evaluator into the picture. However, in the eyes of the project holder, the evaluator has the power to have the proposal funded or not. A responsible evaluator should consciously downplay what proponents perceive as the evaluator's capacity to influence the results of an evaluation study.

People directly involved in the implementation of a project necessarily feel more conversant with the project, in the same way that local evaluators believe they know better about the local situation than their counterparts based in Europe or elsewhere. Since proponents are an evaluator's primary source of data, it is important to maintain open lines of communication with them. Especially problematic is the situation where close bilateral relations between DFAs and proponents existed prior to the evaluator coming into the picture. The evaluator's entry into the process can be perceived as a negative intervention. When this is not properly handled, antagonism on both sides can arise. The creation of communication barriers and obstacles hinders the establishment of rapport between the project holder and evaluator. In such instances, a continuing consultation with the project holder can contribute to a mutually enriching evaluation exercise.

In relation to *the project itself* and the *community* where the project originates, the evaluator assesses the social relevance and technical feasibility of a project. Crucial to this role is the evaluator's ability to understand the project or programme within its broader context. Social development evaluation sees the success of a project in terms of the social change that it has effected. Furthermore one cannot look at a project in isolation from people's lives and culture. Projects are people. Projects must always be understood within the context of the needs and culture of their intended beneficiaries.

For example, years ago the Philippines government decided to build core toilets in an urban resettlement area. The proposal was assessed and the project given the green light. What the evaluator failed to point out was the absence of an education component regarding use of toilet bowls. The result was that the people in the community used the toilet bowls as chairs or flower vases. As one resident acidly pointed out, their main concern was putting food into their stomachs; evacuation was less important.

Credibility to both DFA and proponents is vital if an evaluator is to be effective. One factor in the evaluator's credibility is his or her knowledge of both the technical feasibility and social desirability of the project. Assuring a workable balance between the technical aspects and the social dimension is a continual dilemma and challenge for the evaluator. It may well be, for example, that the welfare of the target population has to be given more weight than a project's technical feasibility. From a humanistic point of view, evaluators may have to exercise more flexibility when assessing the merits of a project. One may even sacrifice some minor technical problems as a trade-off for a long-term positive result which could not be achieved if the particular project were not implemented.

In evaluation it is also important to check the community's perception of the problem against that of the project holder. There are instances when the perceptions are not the same; in such a situation the community's perception should prevail. For example, I once received a well-written proposal for an awareness-raising and organisation project for upland farmers. When I visited the targeted project area, the basic question which the farmers raised was: considering the agro-ecological situation where farms are rainfed and the topsoil is thin, how could they maximise their little piece of land so that it could produce enough food for the table?

To summarise: an evaluator has several roles. To the DFA he or she should be a source of information; to the project holder, a friendly adviser. To both DFA and proponent the evaluator serves as a bridge. And to the project and the community, he or she provides new ideas and alternatives.

Some critical issues for an evaluator

Assuming we agree that evaluation is not merely to do with passing judgements on projects or programmes, but (more importantly) a process of learning and unlearning, of data-gathering and data-giving, and of listening and sharing, then it might be appropriate to review some of the critical issues which have arisen from the many years of evaluation work in the Philippines.

Evaluation process

It would appear that there is now a move away from evaluations performed solely by an external third-party evaluator, to evaluations in which proponents and communities participate in the process. While the merits of a participatory type of evaluation are not difficult to recognise, evaluators are none the less faced with very practical problems such as:

— *Time constraints*: evaluations usually have deadlines to meet. The question to ask is how participative can evaluations become, given the limited time within which they must be undertaken?
— *Cost*: the participation of more people makes the exercise more costly.
— *The capability of the proponent and implementers to participate.* Often there is a need to complement proponents' and implementers' knowledge with some training courses so that they can be equipped with the necessary skills to participate meaningfully in the evaluation process. These added training activities mean that greater cost and longer time are needed in the evaluation.
— A fourth problem, which is applicable to rural Philippines and other parts of Asia as well, is the *culture of silence*. In general Filipinos are not vocal and would prefer to remain silent in gatherings and meetings. Drawing them out and encouraging them to speak their minds is a vital skill for evaluators.

The proponents or the community

Related to the culture of silence is the whole issue of people's culture where the evaluation is taking place. Some implications of this culture include:

1 In the Philippines, as in many countries of Asia, many things are not told or said directly, in order to lessen what might be the negative impact of the statement. The way of communicating is almost always oblique and not straightforward. This is something an evaluator has to be sensitive about; ignoring these *cultural considerations* may render the whole evaluation exercise useless. The simple matter of data-gathering and giving information may become complex when the cultural dimension of the target population is considered. If one does not have the sensitivity to read between and behind the lines, then the information gathered may be limited.

2 *The gender of the interviewer:* a woman respondent may feel more at home answering questions and giving information to a woman evaluator.

3 *The nature of the topic being discussed.* For example, family planning, when taken in a Western context, may spark a lively discussion. In an Asian setting this topic may meet a dead end even before it has got going. Why? In the first place, sex is something not openly discussed in a society where even married couples are very reserved in showing intimacy publicly. A Westerner may find this difficult to comprehend, but an evaluator within such a context has no choice but to recognise this limitation and find creative ways of confronting the issue.

4 *Regional cultural variations:* culture varies not only from country to country, but also from region to region. For example, promoters of organic farming found no difficulty in convincing the Christian farmers of Luzon (the northernmost island of the Philippines) to use animal manure as fertiliser instead of chemical inputs. The same strategy would be resisted by farmers in the southern island of Mindanao, whose religious beliefs prevent them from having anything to do with things considered 'unclean' such as animal manure. Someone insensitive to such cultural beliefs may create setbacks in terms of the project's acceptability by its intended beneficiaries.

5 Another Filipino cultural value which may have a strong bearing on evaluations, whether of a project or a proposal, is *utang na loob*, or sense of indebtedness. A favour given is something one has to recognise and repay for a lifetime. An evaluator who was once indebted to a proponent may find difficulty in assessing the project in an objective manner. To avert problems in this relation, evaluators in the Philippines are not assigned to a project of friends and acquaintances. Besides the embarrassment of telling your friends the weakness of their project, there is the added burden of positive expectations, which may be very high from the other party.

The evaluator

Equally important is the evaluator's consciousness of his or her own values, and how they can be used positively in the evaluation of proposals and projects. While it cannot be denied that the values of the evaluator can influence the direction of a project, the evaluator, who has the power to close down a project, should avoid any tendency to impose his or her personal views. Where the values of the proponent and implementers do not go against the evaluator's, then a smooth evaluation process is more likely to follow. There may be cases, however, when one is faced with three different points of view and values: the proponent's, the DFA's, and the evaluator's. When this happens, it will be important to consider the experiences of other evaluators who have faced the same problem. It is in such situations that dialogue, open communication and trust become exceedingly important.

An evaluator's intervention can have both positive and negative impact. It is up to us, practitioners of social development, to come up with a method of evaluation which can strike a balance between a project's technical aspect and its social merits, which would involve the subject extensively and meaningfully, which will ensure that the project will build on its strengths and minimise its weaknesses, and which can be instrumental in accelerating social development and change. For many of us, evaluation in the past was a 'hit and miss' affair. The challenge for practitioners is to make evaluation both an art and a science. But in order to do this, an evaluator should have the mind of a scientist and the heart of a development activist.

5.2 The evaluator in social development evaluation: Review of workshop papers and discussion

This workshop group addressed the important issue of the appropriate role of the evaluator and his or her position within a re-negotiated evaluation process. In the context of Delle Tiongson-Brouwers' paper, entitled 'The Evaluator in Social Development Evaluation', a number of other papers were presented, which are listed at the end of this chapter. This section summarises the most important issues raised by the group, and elaborates on some issues surrounding the role of the evaluator in social development projects and programmes.

The question of objectivity

Given that objective neutrality is very difficult, if not impossible, to attain, and that an unequal partnership is likely to obtain, the role of the evaluator is extremely difficult to fulfil. According to Tiongson-Brouwers, the evaluator

... should strike a balance between a project's technical aspects and its social merits, so as to ensure that the project will build on its strengths and minimise its weaknesses in order to be instrumental in accelerating social development and change.

Participants were all aware of the dilemmas inherent in devising more qualitative evaluation methods – between the need to search for objectivity and the need to become subjectively involved with the project community. The evaluator is obliged to take on sometimes contradictory roles: an outsider in certain circumstances, and an insider in others. While the idea of the 'armchair evaluator' was generally rejected, it was felt that, under certain circumstances, the information to be obtained through rapid appraisal techniques might be of value. But this has to be complemented by more in-depth studies. Rapid appraisal techniques serve a need for timely and cost-effective collection and dissemination of information, and if they are combined with an attempt to reverse the normal thinking associated with 'expert' intervention, they can be the most effective way of gaining appropriate and useful information. This did, however, raise fundamental questions about who was best for the job. The dilemma was not primarily between the amount of time required for the evaluation, but more about the fundamental rationale for evaluation, which should be seen as an educative process.

The context of evaluation

The social and political environment in which evaluation takes place must be recognised at the outset, for this has implications for the types of evaluations to be carried out and thus for the types of evaluators who may be recruited. The many different actors and their various interests that surround the project community need to be understood if interventions are to have any chance of success. The evaluator plays a potentially important role in negotiating the inevitable compromises that have to be made in this process, and can act as an important bridge between these external influences and the demands and aspirations of the project community.

Different meanings were given to the process of evaluation itself. According to Gary Craig, 'Evaluation is a means of determining the "value" of an organisation or some of its activities or services. It is a term widely used at present to describe a range of processes using different measures to "value" and in a variety of organisational settings.' This definition underlines the problems associated with trying to pin down how evaluations should be undertaken, and by whom. Trying to give a value to certain activities can be a very subjective matter, and depends on where one is standing, within or outside an organisation. But it is the deliberate attempt to avoid subjectivity which, it is assumed, will lead to better forms of assessment, whether they be qualitative or quantitative.

Evaluators as judges

Not only does the evaluator have to attempt to be as objective as possible, but other problems of place and position complicate the process. As an outsider he or she may be perceived as an intruder. Indeed the very essence of traditional evaluations was seen as involving interference by those who knew little of the environment in the internal affairs of those working at the grass roots. Somehow the evaluator has to negotiate a legitimacy which gives credence to his or her work and on which trust can be built in order for effective assessments to be made.

The evaluator can be successful only if all members of the project community participate fully in the process, and a basis of trust is built up between evaluator and evaluand. The question of partiality of knowledge and information gained becomes very important in attempts to obtain a rounded understanding of the many dimensions of social development projects. There are many obstacles to this rounded understanding, not least of which is the political context in which the evaluation takes place.

Drawing on the MYRADA experience in south India, Ranjani Krishnamurthy stressed the difficult and changing role of evaluator over time. As the project moved from planning interventions to supporting initiatives which came from the poor, the nature of evaluation perforce changed. As roles and responsibilities of staff changed, so had their skills, knowledge, and attitudes to be readjusted. Discussion focused on the development and evaluation of a training programme for development professionals. The strengths and weaknesses of this evolving training programme were assessed through the involvement of a variety of different actors with different perspectives on the professional training programme.

Massy Bandera and Anne Buckley in their paper 'The Community Developer and Evaluation' drew attention to the fact that few researchers have really examined the role of the evaluator in any detail. They suggest that community development workers should be given training in self-evaluation and in cultivating powers of observation that would enable them to monitor changes in their own thinking, perhaps through regular entries in a diary, perhaps through regular face-to-face reporting procedures. They argue against the use of external evaluators, on the grounds that they are unlikely to have access to the sorts of qualitative understandings necessary for the interpretation and assessment of particular, context-specific, environments.

The working group identified a series of issues that it felt important to deal with in approaching an understanding of the role of the evaluator:

— The need to classify the types of evaluation in terms of the types of knowledge that each requires.
— The importance of contextualising the evaluator and asking questions about him or her: what interests does she or he have in the knowledge and information being derived from the evaluation?
— The need to recognise that the evaluator has to deal with very different sets of interest groups.
— At a more abstract level, the importance of understanding the different ways in which the knowledge was acquired, and relating this to any implications for the distribution of power: how the knowledge and information is to be used, and by whom.

Participatory evaluation

PROSHIKA's experience with evaluation: Bangladesh

There has been a major change in the way in which PROSHIKA [a Bangladeshi NGO] has undertaken research and evaluation studies. They have moved from being time-bound, need-based, action-oriented, popular activities, to being more deliberately concerned with particular activities. PROSHIKA's understanding of the structural constraints to rural development in Bangladesh was based on the perception of an oppressive agrarian structure. The poor must be organised if any meaningful development is to take place. Various groups at various levels have always been engaged in review and evaluation of programmes. Direct participation of groups in examining issues such as the oppression of women, unjust share-cropping arrangements, money-lending, and patron-client dependency relationships has led to the development of strategies to counter such unequal relationships and to action being taken at very local levels.

Group discussions, inter-group solidarity, alliance building, resource mobilisation and integration, the use of popular theatre, etc. form part of this continuous process of action research. This research and evaluation has been conducted jointly by groups. Objectives of policy formation and strategic decision making have been fulfilled without recourse to sophisticated research/evaluation techniques, or the excessive processing and analysing of large amounts of data written into fat documents for wider circulation.

PROSHIKA maintains coordination forums at three levels which meet at regular intervals to review progress. Area coordinators meet weekly. The coordinators of various programmes meet monthly. Zonal coordinators meet quarterly at the central training centre in Koitta. Such feedback contributes to effective management. Demands for information are met as far as possible using participatory methods, with initiatives arising from open discussions between group members and the 'kormis' (development workers).

(Shahabuddin and Wood 1989)

Social development is about re-arranging the relationships between different social actors, both within and without the project community, in attempts to redefine a new economic and social order. The encouragement of participatory evaluation is seen as one way in which this process might be strengthened. But one of the problems with participation is that it implies cooperation with a structure that has already been established and defined, and the dangers of co-option and incorporation associated with this process need to be highlighted. Evaluation is a deeply political act, and the ramifications of this are very important to understand.

Redefining social reality

The relationship between evaluation and the project cycle has to be examined. The concept of the project cycle is one that incorporates a time framework which is particularly Western, and is worked out in terms of the disbursement of resources, and estimates of time required for disbursements to bear fruit. One of the first lessons that social development has to teach us is that there are many different ways in which the passage of time is perceived, embedded in the culturally specific ways in which value is negotiated. Evaluation then is much more than a mechanistic input at a particular stage in the implementation of a project. It needs to be stripped of its academic baggage in order to make it relevant for people living at the grass roots. The question of how you bring people down to the grass roots becomes an important one, and associated with the general question of whose knowledge counts in an evaluation. But this should not mean that outsiders should necessarily be embarrassed by their role as outsiders. The role of the outsider has traditionally been one of crucial importance in holding up a mirror to practice and in playing the role of intellectual guerrilla or renegade. The outsider is perhaps more able to read between the lines and to turn established and taken-for-granted explanations on their head in the search for a restructured synthesis.

The aim of developing participatory evaluations is to transform traditional judgemental evaluations. To do this it is important to recognise the control that is often exercised through evaluations. While the manifest functions of evaluations are always expressed positively, their latent functions might imply increasing control and increasing dependency. The so-called target populations might end up as victims rather than as beneficiaries of development.

Context-specific nature of work

The characteristics of the organisation will determine the nature of the evaluation, and thus of the evaluator. In most cases the nature of the evaluation is context-specific. In large-scale organisations it may be very formal and involve particular designated workers with particular skills (accountants or external auditors, for example) working to particular briefs and with a set of narrowly defined techniques. In small-scale organisations, where functional specialisation has not developed, it may be completely informal and not subject to written documentation. Evaluation in this context is a generic activity that takes place all the time and is little different from the continuous review of activities that people are engaged in, and which is often dignified with the label of monitoring.

In the middle area between those organisations with special evaluation departments (increasingly in the majority) and those which have no specialist sections, there are one-off evaluations done for particular purposes. Increasingly there is a recognition of the need to maintain an institutional memory that transcends an individual's involvement in a particular project. Such an institutional memory must evolve a structure for communication over time, as well as instruments to ensure communication over a wide set of actors.

The need for evaluations

The need for evaluations stems from a variety of sources. There are at least three different parties that can request evaluations: project donors, evaluation departments and beneficiary groups. This tripartite division can be seen to correspond to an historical development in thinking about evaluations. In the early days of non-government developmental aid, evaluations were sporadic and specialised. Individuals from the organisation or externally recruited professionals were hired on a one-off basis and were usually recruited through personal networks, to report on particular projects. This was not systematic and its purpose was to feed into management ideas that might be useful in explaining failure or lack of achievement and in devising more appropriate strategies for the future.

As the demand for more information grew and the demands for greater accountability intensified, then formal evaluation departments emerged with a remit to systematically collect information on performance and achievement. They thereby created a demand for more systematic evaluations to gain more appropriate types of information, as well as to ensure their own livelihoods. The historical development of evaluation studies is rooted in the work of educationalists and in the need for accredited validation, and in the growth of a separate group of managers responsible for efficiency, effectiveness and economy in their operations. Much has been written in recent years on management by objectives and on the building of institutional commitment through self-assessment procedures.

A third stage was reached when it was recognised that the organisation itself did not have the specialist knowledge to conduct many evaluations, and that in-house studies might not be the most appropriate. External consultants, employed for their objectivity, on contracts, and chosen through 'competitive tendering' were brought in. The evaluation industry burgeoned, producing a specialist, professional group of 'experts' anxious to enshrine a particular type of expertise within professional barriers.

A fourth stage, of incorporating beneficiary evaluations, of putting the people centre stage, is only now being worked out as the boundaries of social development evaluations are explored. It is the elaboration of evaluations at this stage which involves the complete renegotiation of what evaluations can and should be all about.

A more appropriate evaluation framework

Efforts to produce a more appropriate evaluation framework involve the tension between outsiders' and insiders' perspectives, and the tension between the attempts to liberate and to control. Outsiders and insiders possess different sorts of knowledge. Outsiders do not have access to the qualitative understandings that exist at the grass roots, and may be ignorant of or insensitive to local cultural beliefs and traditions. Insiders, on the other hand, may find themselves ensnared in particular, culture-specific frames of reference that fail to take into account the importance of external factors that impact on the performance of the project. It is likely that the struggle to construct a liberating evaluation strategy will be a constant one. Different versions of reality compete for dominance, and attempts to impose a monopoly over explanations need to be constantly countered. Participatory evaluations can be one of the ways in which these monopolies can be challenged.

The workshop drew up a specification for the model evaluator, who would combine knowledge of local cultures with knowledge of evaluation techniques. He or she would be able to generate trust, have empathy with the groups and organisations being studied, recognise the constraints established by the cultural context, both for donors and beneficiaries, and have empathy with the ideology of the organisation. He or she would be committed and capable of coping with difficult and unfamiliar local conditions. An evaluator must be sensitive to local power structures, but must also ensure that information is obtained from non-powerful members of the community: marginalised groups and individuals who rarely get an opportunity to speak.

External evaluators will clearly have problems in fulfilling all of these requirements, but they may be able to play a crucial role as facilitators, and as people who can see things in different ways, allowing others to step out of the blinkered world of everyday, taken-for-granted existence. The biases inherent in most traditional understandings of the project environment, and so vividly emphasised in Robert Chambers' work, need to be understood and made explicit if there is to be any chance of success for participatory evaluations.

Ownership and control of information

The evaluator has to deal with very different sets of interest groups, and significant ethical issues emerge when questions of ownership and use of information are raised. These questions are similar to those raised in any social scientific enquiry, where sensitive information, if falling into the wrong hands, can be turned against those who gave that information, and work against their interests. Professional codes of conduct which protect such enquiries and researchers provide at least some room for manoeuvre. They suggest that formal principles governing inter-relationships between evaluators and their clients may need to be established if there is a danger that evaluators are likely to be co-opted by those who fund their work. Examples of such codes of conduct applicable for evaluators might be elaborated from those currently developed in the fields of chartered accountancy, external and internal auditing. Multiple standards for guiding the work of separate professional evaluators have been elaborated in the USA by the relatively recently established American Evaluation Association.

The evaluator can adopt a number of different roles, depending on the nature of the evaluation considered. Formal, professional types of evaluation are only one sort. When different sorts of information are required, it might be more appropriate if the evaluator is a participant in the project or programme. If this is the case, then evaluation is likely to merge imperceptibly into a process of facilitation. The participant evaluator becomes much more like an *animateur* or a community development worker, operating to clarify tasks and set objectives in the process of project implementation.

Resistance to the evaluator

A major problem that most evaluators have traditionally faced is the resistance to evaluation generally. The perception of evaluators finding fault, looking under stones, bringing out the skeletons in the cupboard is very common, and until appraisal schemes can be viewed as means to self-improvement and the generation of more realistic and practical objectives, they will be viewed with mistrust.

This is obviously intimately connected with the question of legitimacy, especially in terms of external evaluators. There is a fear that the evaluator brings a set of inappropriate values which will inhibit his or her understanding of the real objectives of the project. This is based on a view that an understanding of the dynamics of the project is built up only over a long period of time; the nuances of success and failure cannot be picked up in a few days. The interpretation of success is based on a whole host of contextual characteristics that cannot so easily be observed. In addition to this, project managers might be more concerned with organisational survival than with the particular objectives of a project.

Resources available for the evaluator

The resources available for the evaluator will have a significant bearing on what can actually be achieved. An evaluation demands the expenditure of time and money and unless it is deemed to be legitimate, i.e. valuable in its own right, it is unlikely to be given significant separate status. Some argued that it should be separated as an activity from the ongoing process of information collection and analysis which is part of the managerial task of monitoring. Others argued that in fact the two could not be separated, and evaluation should essentially be seen as a managerial tool, to assist in the more effective negotiation of project objectives.

Whatever the evaluator's position, he or she strongly influences the course of the assessment. Evaluations exist in a political context and cannot really be perceived as neutral activities. The evaluator will build alliances in order to weave a way through the dense reality under investigation. Alliances need to be built, whether one is working as an insider or as an outsider. An insider may be under pressures to adopt a particular stance, to ignore or side-step critical issues, to play down certain issues because they are problematic. The outsider will also be under pressures which will influence judgement: pressure to please the funding agency, pressure to say something original that will distinguish his or her work, pressure to accept the implicit or explicit agenda of the funding agency, pressure to get the job with the most competitive tender.

The working group maintained that evaluation was a process, that it should be participatory and educational, that it has a political context which it is necessary to understand, and that it has costs attached to it if it is to be done successfully. It is, however, the participative element that separates the evaluation of social development projects and programmes from the traditional, more formal cost-benefit, cost-effectiveness analyses. It is the participatory imperative that changes the nature of the evaluation process and inhibits the formal use of techniques which alienate evaluator from evaluand. To be successful, then, evaluation must involve all elements of the project community, and indeed the process of evaluation becomes enmeshed with the process of objective clarification as a mutuality of interest is explored and partnerships developed.

Alienation from development interventions can be circumvented, as workers' alienation from management can, by mutual appraisal which increases a sense of common purpose and collective ownership. Only when people feel themselves to be part of the intervention is sustainability likely to be forthcoming. The problems with the development of appraisal systems are how to design systems that are flexible enough to tolerate many differences of opinion and yet robust enough to remain useful.

Summary and interpretation

Adopting a restructured evaluation framework puts different demands on the evaluator. These demands involve a shift from seeing evaluators as measurers, describers and judges, to seeing evaluators as educators, facilitators, and collaborators. This does not mean that they should abandon the suite of techniques used in formal quantitative assessments, but that these are applied in a different way. Many aspects of social development projects and programmes are not easily measurable, and evaluations of such projects tend to be qualitatively rooted. Rather than being seen as opposed to each other, qualitative and quantitative techniques should be seen as complementary, providing different sorts of interpretations of an ever-changing reality.

Changing purpose of evaluation

With the growth of the organisation there has been a parallel growth in management tasks, and thus in management's need for information. This is being satisfied by a much more sophisticated research and evaluation unit. It is not clear what impact such growth will have on traditional action-oriented participatory research, and there is some feeling that this new development merely serves the interests of external observers/donors, and is more of a ritual than a practical activity.

The need for information comes from donors as well as from academics concerned with documenting PROSHIKA's achievements, and indeed the exchange of information associated with this process is of great importance for internal development. It is however important that PROSHIKA itself do much of this research in order to strengthen its own in-house capacity. PROSHIKA should not be seen as a hunting ground for those who might have better professional skills. Evaluation should serve practical and visible purposes, not remain esoteric studies which retain only ritual significance.

As an NGO with a radical agenda, PROSHIKA attempted to reduce the distance between itself and the group of rural poor with whom it works. This was not easy, even in the beginning, but the educated members of staff still had connections with the rural poor through parents. The organisation was small, and informal, and conscientisation rather than project management dominated the work and ethos of the organisation. The introduction of more formal organisation has changed the culture of the organisation and increased the distance between staff and the groups of rural poor. Pressure to move in this direction has come from external donors, and new staff with even less connection with the groups have been recruited. Renewed efforts will have to be made to ensure that social and cultural distances are not allowed to build up.

But, as the organisation demands increasing specialisations, the informal ethos becomes difficult to maintain. Traditionally the work with the rural poor concerned changing attitudes and social behaviour. These are notoriously difficult to quantify. Slowly the organisation has been drawn through external pressures into measuring that which can be easily quantified. This strengthens the hands of central management and provides reports and figures for outsiders, but does it not undermine the partnership between PROSHIKA and the rural groups? The issues considered important by the rural groups get squeezed out. There is a need to ensure that evaluation activity is so organised to serve the learning needs of the organisation through a more participatory, deprofessionalised, negotiated approach to data collection and management. There is a struggle to maintain the dominance of the populist character of the organisation.

As evaluators we are at a crossroads. On the one hand there are the varied needs of management and intellectuals, on the other hand there are the immediate needs of the organised groups, to identify issues that fundamentally affect their lives, and develop strategies to counter inequalities and oppression. The struggle to maintain a flexible balance between these widely divergent demands is going to be a significant challenge for the future development of the monitoring, evaluation and research unit.

(Shahabuddin and Wood 1989)

The role of evaluator as judge of whether or not objectives have been achieved, or success has been demonstrated, needs to be redefined. The evaluator is one who can draw together the many diverse threads that link the different actors in the process of project development and weave them into a tapestry of inter-relationships. It is not the role of the evaluator to pass judgement, but rather to mediate in the process whereby judgements can be made by the project community.

As emphasised elsewhere in the workshop, evaluation must be an educative process if it is to be valuable within the context of social development projects and programmes. This implies that the evaluator must take on the role of teacher, but not in a didactic way. The different interpretations of reality that inform the views of the various actors in the project community need to be known by all. One of the prime duties of the evaluator is to disseminate these different interpretations. The results of this dissemination process should culminate perhaps in the production of a single text that all can agree to. The authorship of this text rests with the project community rather than with the evaluator, who has merely facilitated its production.

In this latter respect the evaluator is in a powerful position to establish the boundaries by which understandings are arrived at. Giving form to that which was indistinct, unclearly perceived, or only partially formulated is one of the roles that the evaluator can perform in the search for clearer objectives and more realistic assessments. This is a powerful position to be in, because the evaluator can manipulate information and knowledge for particular purposes or for particular actors. On the assumption that the role of evaluation is educative and empowering, then the evaluator takes on the role of *animateur*, feeding into the process information obtained from a whole variety of sources, not available to all members of the project community.

Papers submitted to the working group on the evaluator in social development evaluation

Massy Bandera and Anne Buckley: 'The Community Developer and Evaluation'

Gary Craig: 'The Forbes Trust, Evaluation and Voluntary Organisations'

Ralphy EC-Lumor: 'Evaluation for Project Sustainability: The Motivation and Socio-Cultural Dimensions'

Ranjani Krishnamurthy: 'Evaluation in a Training Programme for Capacity Building of NGOs: Lessons from the Experience of MYRADA'

Hermione Lovell: 'Ten Models of Mothers As Primary Health Care Workers: Which One Are We Using In Our Evaluation?'

Md. Shahabuddin and Geoff Wood: 'The Evaluator in the Evaluation of Social Development Programmes'

SECTION 6

CONCLUSIONS

6.1 Future issues and perspectives

Introduction

Evaluation is important for a variety of reasons. These reasons necessarily reflect the different world views of those approaching the issue, and the changing climate of opinion within the field of development, but are essentially associated with the desire to improve practice and the perceived centrality of processes of evaluation in this process of improvement. Evaluation provides a *key word* (in the sense that Raymond Williams and Ivan Illich talk of key words) around which discussions about more appropriate practice might revolve, and from which a community of interest with a common purpose might evolve. It is important to bear this in mind, given the different motives attributed to the 'negative academic' and the 'positive practitioner', to the distinctions between hard and soft techniques, and to the controversy that still surrounds the notion of objectivity in any discussions about evaluation. All these dichotomies are current in the literature and a hindrance to clear thinking.

In order to make progress in the construction of this more appropriate practice, it is necessary to examine critically the different world views that inform current thinking; to clear away some of the undergrowth that inhibits the growth of new ideas. Rather than taking for granted the often implicit views of others, incorporated into what are seen as authoritative texts, it is important to strip them of their pretensions and point out their partialities as the first step in the construction of purposive actions.

On this basis one might identify two broad approaches to evaluation. Firstly, there is the specific instrumental approach: the desire to know how effective interventions in the name of social development have actually been. This approach might be termed *instrumental/technocratic*. It usually attempts to extend current quantitatively based practices into the new, uncharted seas of social development. Secondly, there is that approach which attempts to confront the dominant instrumental paradigm through an exploration of why evaluations are currently being afforded considerable centrality; to examine the latent functions that evaluations serve, in reinforcing certain sorts of control. This emphasises the political processes involved in evaluations and is not normally characterised by an overt concern with the elaboration of more appropriate practice. For want of a better word, this approach might be term *interpretative*. An interpretative approach provides the basis for what one might call a 'practical' evaluation methodology, something which underpinned much of the thinking of the conference, and something which holds the issues of participation, capacity-building, sustainability, and empowerment as central to the elaboration of more appropriate development strategies.

It is recognised that evaluations are crucial moments in institutional life and are thus deeply political. As crucial moments they offer the opportunities for the reappraisal of practice and the re-formation of objectives, not just at the micro level, but also at the macro level of thinking about the nature of development tasks.

These different approaches are based on distinct ideological premises, or world views. They bring different and separate questions to the analysis of evaluation, and thus engender distinct problematics and distinct programmes for future action. It is important to know where we are coming from if we are to chart successfully our course for the future.

The instrumental/technocratic approach to evaluation

If one adopts an instrumental or technocratic approach, then the deeply political nature of evaluations may remain unaddressed. Literature on these instrumental/technocratic bases is rich. It is this literature that represents the dominant paradigm within the field of evaluation studies, as pointed out in Peter Oakley's overview paper on the Evaluation of Social Development. It is fundamentally linked with that school of management which perceives the management task as the development of rationally designed and operational tools for the realisation of predominantly instrumental objectives. It is informed by a belief in the value-neutrality of Western scientific methods and by the objectivity which their correct utilisation will facilitate. It is deeply rooted in the functionalist tradition within the social sciences. Evaluation in this context is supposed to increase managerial control through the systematic coordination of social action, and the use of a set of neutral techniques and methods. The elaboration of these methods and techniques is based on a systems approach to the analysis of organisations, and assumes that more effective coordination and increased order and control can be achieved through progressive fine tuning of the technical instruments used in evaluations. A 'blueprint' for successful implementation will eventually be available.

Evaluations of this latter type assume that quantification will proceed and be enhanced as subjectivity is minimised and as certainty about discrete activity develops; objectives will be progressively clarified and, as they become so, the ability to assess, count, compare and weigh will also be enhanced. Typical exponents of this approach may indicate that we are in the early stages of understanding how to evaluate social development projects, but with more and more information available, the uncertainty that currently attaches to them will progressively disappear. There is a trust in the ability to overcome uncertainty eventually.

Evaluation in this context is primarily a tool of management used to attempt to gain increased control. Such control is seen as a natural prerogative of management and as essential for the effective implementation of policies, and for the organisation of institutions. The political and historical contexts in which such control is exercised essentially remain outside the equation. Evaluation is reduced to a static and mechanical operation designed to point out irrationalities, inconsistencies, and bad practices, in pursuit of the ideal organisational form. As such it should come as no surprise that evaluators and evaluations are cast in a negative light and that evaluations of this type are regarded with suspicion.

The investigation should be done by outsiders who can, because of their distance (intellectual, physical and emotional) retain 'objectivity'. Evaluators are agents for a formal and instrumental rationality who focus on design faults. Appraisal, monitoring, and evaluation activities demand separate treatment at different stages in the project cycle. Evaluators embody a professional expertise characterised by detachment and scientific rigour. There is an evolving professional code of practice which echoes that established for auditors and accountants in the business world. They pursue the 'naturalised' goals of economy, efficiency, and effectiveness — the hallmarks of modern managerialism and the banners of the new Right. We say 'naturalised' because those goals are seen as self-evident and remain unquestioned. There is no account taken of the fact that they are imbued with values which are culturally and ideologically specific. Their aims are essentially to minimise costs and maximise benefits in the pursuit of profitability. The values of capitalism are to be extended into public sector investment programmes by the establishment of proxy measures for profit, established through cost centres and the development of more competitive practices.

Arising from a formal and functionalist tradition, such instrumental methods encounter problems when it comes to measuring the impact of social development projects and programmes. Attempts to deal with such projects and programmes which often have indistinct objectives, or objectives that are highly abstract (such as enhancing citizen participation, increasing solidarity, building institutional capacity) have led to the search for more appropriate and more exact indicators for social development. The emphasis has been on trying to clarify objectives so that achievements can be measured. Much of the work of the United Nations Research Institute for Social Development, for example, has been geared to the search for more sophisticated indicators which will measure the less tangible advances which are deemed to be at the heart of effective development. In the last decade or so the development of instruments for Rapid Rural Appraisal, for example, and of other proxy measures for achievement have attempted to enhance our understanding of the process of development, and broaden the scope of this instrumental tradition. But they have remained, by and large, rooted in the paradigm that assumes that the more information you have, the easier it will be to make decisions, and the sooner the solutions for more effective development will be forthcoming; or, if there is not enough time to collect sufficient information, then there is a need to ensure that you can identify reliable proxies for the information that you otherwise might have gathered. They demonstrate that it is indeed possible to get good and relatively reliable information in a time-efficient manner which satisfies the objective demands of legitimate scholarship and the demands of managers who require their information yesterday.

This approach to evaluation in terms of human engineering assumes that the values of those initiating traditional evaluative studies are widely accepted and internalised; they have become part of the 'naturalised' and 'taken-for-granted' world. What have been called 'quick' and 'dirty' techniques are legitimised because of the need for timely reports, to feed into the decision-making process. They are not thereby opposed to 'long' and 'clean' techniques that are supposedly better, and associated with traditional scholarship. They are, rather, extensions of the same methods, but focused on an increased instrumentality. Research itself has to bow before the constraints (and opportunities) provided by the quest for the three Es (Efficiency, Effectiveness, and Economy), and the demands of project managers and donors. If they are seen as oppositional, then a false dichotomy is set up between what are regarded as the positive practitioners and the negative academics (the persons who supposedly sit on the side lines and offer nothing more than criticism). This dichotomy is echoed in the dichotomy that is created between qualitative and quantitative sorts of information, and in the mystifying hard/soft, pure/applied divisions within social sciences generally.

It should be added that this approach to evaluation is underpinned by ideologues who insist that the liberal democratic tradition, with its emphasis on competition in a free market, is the natural end-product of the process of development. The industrial democracies offer the only sane and viable approach to global peace and prosperity. This is given added poignancy by the apparent failure of 'communist' systems around the world. As Francis Fukuyama, a US Deputy Under-Secretary of State for Policy Planning, put it in *The National Interest* No.16 (Summer 1989):

> What we may be witnessing is not just the end of the cold war, or the passing of a particular period of post-war history, but the end of history as such: that is the end point of mankind's ideological evolution and the universalization of western liberal democracy as the final form of human government.

The interpretative approach

A second approach to evaluation that is described here is called interpretative in order to link it to those interpretative sociologies which place subjectivity at the centre of the experience of culture and history, and thereby call into question the whole project of functionalist, positivistic social science. They are here associated with the work of people like Berger, Bailey, Goffman, Illich, Bourdieu, Schaffer, Apthorpe, and Douglas. In the Development literature this approach is associated with what have been described as the 'negative academics' and, for those who regard themselves as 'positive practitioners', many of its findings are not regarded as particularly helpful; they are dismissed as inappropriate for those involved with development projects, untimely, or riddled with jargon. Such an attitude to this approach polarises discussion in an unhelpful way. On the one hand there are seen to be the pure and objective scientists, who pursue esoteric research topics, or topics which have no obvious relationship to practical concerns. As such, they fail to engage with the dynamics of development policy implementation. On the other hand, there are applied scientists whose work is supposed to be specifically associated with policy analysis and development administration, who engage with the real world in an attempt to make sense of it for the policy makers and the administrators.

At the risk of overstating the case, 'negative academics' are dismissed as unable to engage with the 'real' world of development practice and can thus be marginalised from development activities. They are not able to speak in a language that is intelligible or useful to the policy makers and the project administrators. They raise uncomfortable questions about motives for intervention and the purposes attributed to particular actors and actions. They are not able to make strategic interventions in the project cycle, because they tend to focus on issues that are tangential to the requirements of managers.

It could be argued that this polarisation between 'pure' and 'applied' is unhelpful. The debate tends to collate and confuse several sets of distinctions that are currently central to thinking about social development projects and programmes and their evaluation. Clarity in addressing them separately and placing them in the overall scheme of thinking about the interpretative approach to evaluation might help in the charting of a more appropriate course of action. A number of distinctions need to be highlighted and considered separately, rather than lumped together into an overgeneralised and relatively crude dichotomy, as they so often are in the popular imagination; a dichotomy which emphasises the distinction between pure and applied research. These sets of distinctions, like the different approaches to evaluation themselves, are perhaps overdrawn, but this is done in order to focus attention on them.

One distinction is between *academic* and *practical* work. In modern Western society, until comparatively recently, the former was to be found in specialised institutions (universities) and was seen, for better or for worse, as conceptually distinct from the latter, which was carried on outside universities. This intellectual division of labour was predicated on a certain understanding of the nature of academic enquiry — separate, objective, pure — which no longer holds (although like Modernisation Theory its legacies continue to misinform understanding).

The second distinction is between *objectivity* and *subjectivity*. As traditional academic enquiry became increasingly aligned with objectivity, so the 'pure' became increasingly associated with the 'objective', and a certain form of enquiry was disassociated from its roots in practical reality. Reflection was disassociated from action, as pure objective enquiry struggled to gain a monopoly over legitimate knowledge. The 'pure' and 'objective' research, untainted with the need to answer to any constituency other than its own, was considered as somehow inferior.

A third set of distinctions needs also to be drawn. This is between ideologues who assume what can broadly be described as *Marxist perspectives* on the nature of development, and those who are champions of a *free market economy*. The former have tended to reject anything which smacks of capitalist penetration, in favour of what they deem to be socialist development strategies. The latter, certainly in recent years, have tended to assert the overriding benefits that in their view will accrue from participation in a free market economy, and which derive from the encouragement of individual initiative and enterprise.

A fourth set of distinctions, which are connected to the ideological debates about the role of the state and the direction for economic development, are those to be made between the *individual* and the *community*, as the limits to government are currently being renegotiated. A focus on the individual favours the pursuit of individual goals, and is associated with authors such as Hayek. A focus on the community favours the development of community responsibility for the production and maintenance of public assets. The struggle between those who advocate increased private responsibility and those who advocate increased public welfare provision is central to many of the current debates about structural adjustment. The struggle here is particularly germane to the work of non-government agencies, as those who recommend the retraction of government support put increased emphasis on provision through the private voluntary sector.

A fifth set of distinctions that also needs to be emphasised is the distinction between *sociology* and *economics*. Economics, or perhaps more precisely neo-classical economics, has gained a pre-eminent position within the social sciences as the discipline that is able to address itself most directly, and with the most precise tools, to the central concerns of development practice. Sociology, by contrast, has been relegated to an inferior position: little more than the application of common sense, when it is not tarred with the brush of subversion. 'Practical' considerations are popularly linked with economics, representing the apparently most practical of the social sciences, and certainly the subject which has managed to generate the most legitimacy in the field of development planning. By default, this association tends to increase the connections that are made in the lay person's eyes between the 'theoretical' and 'ideal' considerations which are linked with the apparently least practical of the social sciences, sociology. The myth of the separation between the social and the economic is thereby enhanced; the one is associated with specialism, the other with generalism.

Questioning legitimacy

The interpretative approach to evaluation is then about resisting the formal claims to legitimacy and authority that are made by those who claim to have expert knowledge. It is also about questioning those interpretations of the world that have appeared as natural, about reading between the lines, and about standing established explanations on their heads, so that we can see things differently and perhaps a little more clearly: the Indians discovered Columbus; all gifts are poisonous; doctors create disease; participation is co-option; decentralisation is essentially about extending the power of the centre; the quest for equality is illusory. Authority and legitimacy are constantly questioned in a critical evaluation of the taken-for-granted world. Nothing escapes the purview of an interpretative evaluation, which is primarily aimed at deconstruction.

There is a distinct shift of focus associated with the interpretative approach. The place of structure as something into which individuals can be pigeon-holed so that they are deemed to be playing roles rather than acting as individuals gives way to a much more flexible interpretation of the knowing subject constructing reality in terms which are much less given and much more plastic. The interpretative approach deliberately tries to look at the other side of the coin. In doing this, its exponents have often been accused of doing nothing but deconstructing established explanations. This aspect of their work has led to the belief that all their work is negatively oriented. While an account of the sort of work they have been doing here tends to over-state their negative impact, the interpretative approach contains a rich tradition from which valuable insights have emerged which have helped in understanding the complexities of the development process, and a rich foundation on which policy makers have constructed more appropriate strategies for intervention. It has highlighted the complex inter-relationships that exist between theory and practice and between reflection and action. It is important to recuperate many of these insights into a re-oriented view of evaluation that needs to be enhanced if evaluations are to be developed as learning exercises.

Evaluations are never neutral

An interpretative approach to evaluation assumes that truth is relative, that evaluations can never be neutral, and that they are fundamentally about control over direction and resources. The rhetorical devices used by development practitioners often disguise different motives which are often designed to accomplish exactly the opposite of what the public statements suggest they will accomplish. Participation may be more about incorporating outlying populations into a particular system of government than about giving power to the people. The public pursuit of equity might provide more opportunities for elites to capture the benefits of development and result in even greater differences in wealth than currently apply. The 'good faith' employed by public or private agencies in pursuit of what is termed 'the common good' may be merely a means of promoting individual interests and ensnaring people into processes over which they have little control and from which they may stand to lose a considerable amount, in terms of resources as well as in terms of independence. As is patently obvious, the manifest functions of development projects often have very negative and unintended consequences; these the interpretative analyst is at pains to point out.

From this point of view a project of Social Development is an ideological apparatus aimed at mitigating the extreme effects of mass poverty, and avoiding major structural changes through the encouragement of what are merely diversionary tactics. Those who are in control of resources retain that control, and the hegemony of Western cultural categories, however embroidered with multi-cultural and multi-racial epithets, however aware of indigenous aspirations, however committed to the advancement of cultural pluralism, is enhanced. Domination is assured by a form of cultural imperialism which is more sophisticated than the crude imperialism backed by armed force. The expression that 'the pen is mightier than the sword' fails to address the question of who uses the pen, and who creates the word which is written. As Eric Wolf has so admirably demonstrated, it was the people of Europe who wrote the history of the world; it was they who 'discovered' America and Africa! Knowledge is often taken from people and used in counter-productive ways. A sophisticated cultural hegemony controlled by those with resources ensures the incorporation of marginal areas of the world into a world system dominated by the North. However much the poor are allowed to speak, they can do so only through the microphones of the rich.

Levels of interpretative evaluation

The main aim of the interpretative approach to evaluation is to address the issue of power. This is done at a number of different levels and with a number of constituencies:

1 *The project:* At the level of the project, the major concern is to unravel the politics of distribution of resources, by identifying those individuals who are able to capture and divert benefits which are targeted on particular groups — for example poor women, or landless labourers. It also aims to expose the ways in which resources accrue differentially to different groups, through an historical and political appreciation of how relationships of inequality become established and legitimated. A good example of this sort of evaluation is afforded by the investigations of power networks in rural Bangladesh undertaken by the Bangladesh Rural Advancement Committee (BRAC).

2 *Project management:* At the level of project management, the main aim is to expose the ways in which resource allocation processes are manipulated by 'non-rational considerations', related to sectional interests and values, and motivated by what have been termed the 'politics of affection' (Hyden). It is assumed that rationality is dominated by considerations of short-term political and financial advantage, and individual gains associated with status improvement. A major aim of this sort of evaluation is to expose corruption, paternalism, and nepotism. By stripping off the cultural layers that hide 'bad practice', the stage is set for the elaboration of more honest, just, and egalitarian strategies. A good example of this sort of evaluation study is provided by Wade's analysis of corruption in South India (Wade 1984).

This sort of evaluation of project management can be extended to an examination of internal dynamics, by exposing sectional and special interests, cliques and networks which operate to divert organisational interests into individual preoccupations, and thus subvert the manifest aims of the project. Such an evaluation aims to understand how order is negotiated within the organisation, on the assumption that the rules and regulations that govern hierarchy, procedures, and monitoring and recording techniques are not static or immutable but can be manipulated by particular people for particular interests. It also aims to discover the sources of tension and disagreement within the organisation so that these might be removed and an organisational culture working with a common ideal might be fostered. The aim of such an evaluation is deemed to be the improvement in the political skills of those who manage such organisations; to equip themselves with the (Machiavellian?) skills necessary to control more effectively. Studies of this kind are few and far between, but see Marsden 1989 for an organisational study of a Community Development Department which was the lead agency in a slum improvement project in India. Such evaluations can be extended to include donor organisations, but they are not common and, because of their sensitivity, tend to produce internal documents which have only restricted circulation.

Tackling related issues, Des Gasper (1987) argues for the construction of a 'sociology of assessment'. He builds up the contrasts between practitioners and assessors, and between insiders and outsiders, and lays out the dimensions of what he calls the 'goals clarification game'. He argues that programme evaluations tend to be negatively biased, and he investigates the limits of trust that are perceived to be vital in the development of an effective evaluation. He examines the internal management battles to control assessment from a point of view which exposes the individual prejudices of the actors involved, and which assumes self-seeking as a major motivating factor. He does not, however, take us very far in the analysis of the programme environment, nor in the analysis of moral responsibility, but as an analysis of the dynamics of internal management, his argument is very useful.

3   *The project environment:* But there is a macro- (or contextual) level at which interpretative evaluations are also important. At this macro-level there is a need to understand the socio-political context in which the agency is operating and in which it is also embedded, in order to understand more effectively what can and what cannot work, and in order to lobby more effectively for resources or recognition. An effective evaluation of the party or parties which is/are most likely to have an influence on the development of particular courses of action might uncover novel ways of influencing individuals and of creating a climate of public opinion more conducive to the expansion of agency ideals. What

sorts of media opportunities are there? What types of message are likely to receive more favourable attention? Who might be identified as spokespeople? What sorts of coalitions need to be built in order for intervention strategies to be more effective? What sorts of competitors are likely to be pursuing the same sorts of objectives? What sorts of opposition is the project likely to encounter? An evaluation of the external environment before the implementation of projects (what in business might be termed 'market research') might facilitate the speedy implementation of the project and enhance its perceived legitimacy. This evaluation should not be confined just to pre-project stages, but should be a feature of all stages. This is no less a part of the evaluation process than attempts to measure whether resources committed have been used effectively and efficiently, but it has usually been associated with some form of monitoring.

Associated with the analysis of the project environment is the analysis of what has been termed 'development discourse', or the language in which development issues are expressed. An understanding of this language enables the evaluator as well as the project management (if they are different) to understand the room for manoeuvre that exists in particular social and political circumstances. There are at least four aspects to the study of development discourse that need to be isolated for students of interpretative evaluation, all associated with being able to 'speak truth to power' in one way or another.

Firstly there is that discourse aimed at decreasing the distance between academics and others which surrounds the differential and derogatory use of the term 'jargon'. Secondly there is that discourse which is aimed at opening social and political 'spaces' for the development of ambiguous complementarity; a discourse aimed at providing room for manoeuvre in situations where legitimate opposition is repressed and public discussion on certain issues is foreclosed; where freedom fighters are labelled guerrillas, where public ownership is deemed wasteful, where labour unions are deemed harmful to the public interest, where socialists are labelled as subversives, and also where capitalists are labelled as decadent, for example. Thirdly there is the analysis of that discourse between different constituencies within the project community. Fourthly and more abstractly is that discourse which challenges existing interpretations, by demonstrating their foundations in particular times and places, and their associations with particular interest groups.

Precise ideas need precise formulation. The different social sciences and the different professions have developed specialist vocabularies for particular reasons. While this vocabulary might seem impenetrable to those outside the discipline or profession, it has been developed to deal with important features that need clarification or precision. A knowledge of this special vocabulary takes time to learn, as the knowledge of any new language does. A common cry, especially from the 'positive practitioner' is that this 'scientific' language mystifies and obfuscates the reality that it is supposed to clarify. But to dismiss it automatically as jargon is to fall into the traps laid by those who would separate the universities and the professions from the social realities in which they are embedded. It is equivalent to perceiving any other language as inferior, and to consigning any other interpretation of events to insignificance.

While we could argue for more precision and less ambiguity in the description and analysis of social reality, this is not an argument for the automatic retention of separate languages. The issue of jargon echoes the issues surrounding the position of the insider or the outsider, and the distinctions made between the expert and the generalist. Critics might well castigate specialists whom they fail to understand, or of whom they are jealous, or whose privileges they wish to question. This seems to be perfectly legitimate. Illich, more than others, has exposed the dangers associated with the acceptance of the privileged vocabularies of others and the monopolies over established explanations that arise therefrom.

When a specialist language is associated with and perpetuates asymmetrical social and political relationships, then it needs to be questioned. Deference and unthinking respect for established authority, while widespread, are not necessarily tolerable for those involved in interpretative evaluations. If one of the chief aims of social development projects is the development of critical consciousness, then the deconstruction of the special privileges associated with control over language must be one of its principal objectives. A key element in the construction of a practical evaluation must be the analysis of the words used by the participants in the project community. The emphasis on the production of a single evaluation text, in whatever form, focuses attention on this process. The methodologies developed by Paulo Freire for adult literacy programmes are as relevant to the processes of evaluation as they are to the acquisition of literacy.

When professionals and academics use their specialist knowledge to perpetuate privilege and monopolise use and control of this knowledge, then the need for deconstruction becomes apparent, and the need to ensure that the non-establishment, non-professional voice is heard, and that serious attempts are made to speak to a whole variety of different audiences in pursuit of a more holistic and perhaps more workable truth.

Understanding what is said

The art of being able to speak truth to power is not one that is monopolised by the evaluator. It is an art to be found at all levels in the project community. Recipients of aid will match their language to that which they expect the donor to understand. This inhibits effective communication, if effective communication is about building up a dialogue based on mutual trust. Those who express a willingness to participate in a project have already identified themselves as willing, and perhaps able, to speak the language of the donor, and thereby to take part in something which is outside the normal course of their lives. In cultures where respect for established authority and deference to age and position are important ways in which interactions between people are regulated, then cutting through the impenetrable layers that mask real individual motives may be extremely difficult. Understanding these private aspirations, negotiating more truthful positions, revealing hidden relationships, and exposing the mechanisms which perpetuate structural inequality in order to enhance more egalitarian cooperation are essential prerequisites for enhancing partnership and creating a basis for the empowerment of the hitherto excluded as well as undermining an inegalitarian *status quo*. But they are also the basis for the imposition of a particular way of viewing the world; even in the pursuit of social development objectives, the dangers of cultural imperialism are ever-present.

An interpretative evaluation will assert that people always tell you what it is they think you want to know, rather than the 'truth'. They will attempt to speak a language that you can understand, but they will also speak a language of compromise, depending on who they think you are and the expectations that they have about the nature of continuing relationships (if any). An interpretative evaluation is alert to these partial revelations and to the places that people occupy or perceive themselves to occupy in the project community. Different sorts of people will be able to obtain different sorts of information. The information that an outside evaluator can obtain is only one sort of information. Other, equally valuable sorts of information may remain hidden. The problem with the interpretative evaluation is that it can never make judgements; while recognising the sanctity of different positions, it remains locked in the trap of cultural relativity.

Thus, according to the interpretative evaluator there are different ways of seeing, and it is up to policy makers to decide which is the most appropriate. If they wish to incorporate these different ways of seeing into the policy process through the encouragement of participatory practices without clear objectives, but in the interests of pursuing an indigenous development strategy, then they are sailing through uncharted waters.

The project planner does not come to the project without ideological and theoretical baggage. He or she already has structured categories by which the world is interpreted. One role for the interpretative evaluator is to explore the nature of this baggage. Different sorts of people are labelled in different ways and then isolated for separate treatment. Landless labourers are separated from their brothers who are small-scale farmers. Women are isolated from their families. Elites are isolated from the communities over which they have authority. Tribes are isolated and given separate definition in terms of their evolving interaction with an emerging nation state (see Godelier 1976). The closure of national boundaries isolates people as refugees.

In the interests of reaching the poorest of the poor, through selective targeting, people are stigmatised by being labelled. Poverty then becomes a privilege; in order to receive benefits one has to establish membership of a particular category (scheduled caste, scheduled tribe, economically weaker section, to use examples from India; unemployed, social security recipient, homeless, to use categories from the West). Such membership may have the effects of decreasing social mobility and of increasing social control. Labelling people keeps them in their place, but that place is circumscribed by those who adopt very partial views of the world. As Illich points out, 'Tribal people who hardly have any needs will turn into "beggars" who begin to expect something because they are "poor"' (Illich 1981).

Challenging existing interpretations

Labelling theory contains a rich body of information on ways in which stigma is attached to particular categories of people, and the domesticating effects that this can have (see Schaffer 1982). People are marginalised into pre-conceived categories. Interpretative studies of culture and history which explore the structuring of reality and knowledge are an important part of contemporary social science research. A background to the debates which currently inform social development thinking about the nature of evaluation may be found in a variety of different sources. A history of the ways in which power and knowledge have structured the growth of particular social institutions in the West and contributed to the separation of people into different categories is provided in the work of people like Michel Foucault (1984) and Ivan Illich, whom we have mentioned before. A history of the ways in which people of the Third World have been perceived by Westerners is provided in the work of people like Ignacy Sachs (1987). An analysis of how different cultural premises structure organisational form and direction is to be found in the work of people like Mary Douglas (1986).

An evaluation of the respective positions of the different constituencies within the project community is a pre-requisite for the initiation of any project. For the interpretative evaluator this means giving much more central importance to the analysis of history and of culture if significant insights are to be afforded.

Finally, but perhaps significantly, when examining the interpretative approach to evaluations, one cannot escape the conclusion that 'evaluation' as a separate category cannot exist. It is inextricably tied to the negotiation of value and the structuring of knowledge. People evaluate all the time. It is not a separate activity. From their evaluation of particular activities comes an understanding of effectiveness as well as the methodologies that they employ. People evaluate by not participating, by doing things in a certain sort of way, by committing resources and a certain amount of time to an activity. These things can be measured relatively easily. What cannot be measured so easily are the intellectual tools and the cultural and historical baggage that they bring to that activity which make them behave in the ways in which they do. Interpretative evaluations can clarify the limits to understanding that exist, they can critically appraise current practice, and they can begin to offer a way forward.

Conclusion

The way forward, as underlined by many of the contributions to the conference, lies in the construction of a practical evaluation that embodies many of the central concerns of an interpretative enquiry. But one of the very serious assumptions under which interpretative evaluations labour is that of the cultural relativity which their emphasis on subjectivity forces them into. While the sanctity of different cultural interpretations is maintained, no mechanism exists to construct or impose a meta-interpretation based on an over-arching morality. The dangers of this are manifold. Firstly, those who have less compulsion to respect cultural differences can proceed unchecked in the advancement of their particular projects, based on dogmatic beliefs in their own mission (free-market capitalists, for example, or fundamentalist Muslims). Secondly, a realisation of the partiality of Western knowledge, and the associated guilt occasioned by past imperialist ventures, immobilise many well-intentioned liberals, and disable many very worthwhile development interventions. And, thirdly, as a result of this paralysis, accusations of paternalism, elitism, and racism remain unchallenged. The Western liberal establishment gives the stick to others, who are allowed to brandish it and beat the indecisive cultural relativist: the tail begins to wag the dog.

Also associated with this assumption of cultural relativism and the central importance given to subjectivity in interpretative evaluations is the confusion that surrounds the notion of 'belonging'. This gets bound up with the issue of objectivity, as well as with the issue of control. To 'belong' to something, a community, a group, or an organisation, puts one on the inside. As an insider one is privy to information which is not available to the outsider. One will always believe that one's information about what is going on in one's group is superior to any information which the outsider might have. Those who maintain a relativist and subjective viewpoint in the interpretation of cultural values must agree: the insider is the ultimate subject. They must also agree that it is not possible for the outsider ever really to gain entry. Herein lie other dilemmas for the evaluator who would adopt an interpretative approach. The desire of the interpretative evaluator to ensure that people remain the subjects of their own world, rather than the objects of other people's worlds, excludes the possibility of objective analysis. How can he or she then put a value on the activities of the group under study?

A way that has been suggested is through *participant observation*, where it is assumed that intensive interaction with the group over an extended peiod of time will provide 'inside information'. This 'inside information' is derived from key informants (a term that in other contexts has distinctly pejorative overtones: one who reveals things that he or she is not supposed to). Many studies testify to the marginal nature of these key informants. How long does one have to stay with a group before one really knows it: two months, ten years? How long does one have to stay with a group before one can impute values to the activities one is observing? Who can be considered to be insiders? The marginal informants who are so eager to relate to the foreigner? The urban nationals who claim to be able to represent the views of their rural 'brothers and sisters'? The foreign anthropologist who has spent one or two years with the group? The governmental extension officer who deals only with the elite? The representative of the women's league, whose husband is the village headman? Or the consultant who has been in the area for only a few weeks? All have their own interpretations based on the cultural baggage they carry to the reality being observed. All are partial, and all the information that they possess can be used under prescribed circumstances.

Interpretative evaluations and the building of cultural and organisational identity

The issue of control emerges in questions about 'belonging' when one begins to ask who gives expression to group identity. Current managerial interests in the development of corporate cultural images focus on the encouragement of a sense of belonging to encourage allegiance to company policy. Rituals of association are elaborated which bind employees into something more than a paid job. The success of Japanese corporations in ensuring loyalty and in building internal consensus is well known. From a critical point of view one could argue that this is merely an attempt to draw a veil over the essentially exploitative relationship that governs the extraction of surplus value involved in capitalist development, and delivers profits to the owners and wages to the workers. The building of a corporate identity is then a management tool to ensure greater control. The issue of trust and mutual confidence is crucial to this task.

While these aims are laudable in themselves, they must, according to the interpretative evaluator, be considered in context, and the issue of control is never a neutral issue. It usually means the dominance of one particular set of values over another, and the fact that in this instance these are management's values should not mean that they are above criticism. The achievement of legitimacy and authority is something that should not be taken for granted.

But what of non-government organisations which are neither capitalist corporations nor large-scale public bureaucracies? Can they be analysed in the same critical way? While recognising that it is difficult to generalise about the features of NGOs, given their extreme heterogeneity, an apparent feature of such organisations involved in development is the common sense of purpose that their members maintain: a trust in the legitimacy of their mission. This cohesion is seen as something positive, which distinguishes them from those large-scale bureaucratic agencies which are unable to develop in their employees a sense of close personal identity with the aims of the agency. In NGOs this sense of common purpose seems a prerequisite to membership, while in large organisations it is something that has to be intensively worked at. In the former the spirit of volunteerism is all-pervasive. So are they any different from other organisations? In their internal dynamics probably not, but in their approach to the achievement of their objectives, there may be significant differences which influence the ways in which their performance might be evaluated. The flexible and adaptable ways in which they are supposedly able to work, the lack of rigidity and formality in their work practices, and the considerable degree of initiative they allow to individuals suggest that the issue of control is a different one.

But is this in fact true? Modern management practice is dominated by contingency theory: the idea that there is no best way to manage or to organise, and that organisations should gear themselves to constant adaptation, both internally and externally. Current thinking in this 'post-Fordist' era is to disassemble large-scale monolithic organisations in favour of smaller more flexible units which are related to parent institutions through contractual arrangements. But in disassembling these large-scale units, one is also disassembling the structures which provided security for their members. The rules and regulations which governed such organisations are a two-edged sword. They may have discouraged initiative, but they also protected employees against the arbitrary dictates of management. What is the situation inside non-governmental organisations? An interpretative evaluation of the social development programme which here is the NGO, with a focus on these issues, remains to be written. But it might be argued that a significant feature of employment in many such organisations is the large turn-over of staff, *en route* to better opportunities, and the external resources that many individuals possess which cushion them against relatively poor remuneration. It makes it very important, therefore, to situate these non-governmental organisations within a much more general socio-political environment; they are not so separate as is often imagined.

Solidarity with the poor

The analysis of commitment to and involvement in the activities of a small organisation can be more easily circumscribed than the analysis of commitment to and solidarity with the poor and oppressed of the world. And yet for many NGOs the latter is a key objective, and one of the major aims of exploring strategies for a more practical evaluation methodology is to work out more effectively how this key objective might be accomplished.

A practical evaluation of this extension of the notion of belonging must start again from the issues of control and empowerment. If this is not addressed in a renegotiated evaluation effort, then evaluations can never be seen as learning exercises, and are always about the continued extension of another form of cultural hegemony.

The asymmetry inherent in the relationship between donor and recipient is self-evident, however much it is moderated by intermediaries and intermediate organisations. The idea of partnership in development, while attempting to overcome this hierarchical and dependent asymmetry, is in danger of exacerbating it if it does not overcome the false dichotomy between insider and outsider, and the myth of equality, and begin to recognise what Illich calls the 'ambiguous complementarity' that must be nurtured between people involved in social development (Illich 1982:70). This ambiguous complementarity is seen here as equivalent to that which exists between men and women, or between left and right. Separate and distinct identities should be given to complementary aspects of social life, like the complementary relationships that exist between nomads and cultivators, between rural and urban dwellers, between professionals and lay people, and perhaps between donors and recipients of aid.

For a renegotiated evaluation methodology these complementarities must be elaborated, and the socio-political foundations on which evaluations are based must be clarified. For evaluations to become instruments for liberation and tools for empowerment — liberating, rather than domesticating, activities — they must transcend the old dichotomies which separate subjective from objective, and which consign insiders and outsiders to separate sides of the fence. The conference went some way in preparing an agenda for more practical and useful evaluations, but much work remains to be initiated in this area, as well as in the wider inter-relationships which govern the development of donor-beneficiary complementarity in an ever-changing world.

Bibliography

Bryant, C. and L.G. White (1982), *Managing Development in the Third World*, Boulder, Colorado: Westview Press.

Cernea, M. (1985), *Putting People First: Sociological Variables in Rural Development*, Oxford: Oxford University Press.

Chambers, R. (1978), *Rural Poverty-Orientated Monitoring and Evaluation*, Brighton: Institute of Development Studies, University of Sussex.

Chambers, R. (1983), *Rural Development: Putting the Last First*, Harlow: Longman.

Chavunduka, D.M. et al. (1985), *Kuluma Usenza, the Story of ORAP in Zimbabwe's Rural Development*, Bulawayo.

Cook, T.D. and C.S. Reichardt (eds.) (1979), *Qualitative and Quantitative Methods in Evaluation Research*, Beverley Hills: Sage.

Damadaram, K. (1988), 'The Qualitative Evaluation of Rural Social Development', unpublished MA dissertation, University of Reading.

Dasgupta, S. (1986), *Forest, Ecology and the Oppressed*, New Delhi: People's Institute for Development and Training.

Douglas, M. (1986), *How Institutions Think*, London: Routledge Kegan Paul.

Esman, M.J. and N. Uphoff (1984), *Local Organizations: Intermediaries in Rural Development*, Ithaca, NY: Cornell University Press.

Foucault, M. (1970), *The Order of Things: An Archaeology of the Human Sciences*, London: Tavistock.

Gasper, D. (1987), 'Motivations and manipulations: some practices of project appraisal and evaluation', *Manchester Papers on Development* 3/1, March 1987.

Godelier, M. (1976), *Perspectives in Marxist Anthropology*, Cambridge: Cambridge University Press.

Hardiman, M. and J. Midgley (1982), *The Social Dimensions of Development: Social Policy and Planning in the Third World*, Chichester: Wiley.

Howes, M. et al. (1984), *Assessing Rural Development Projects: An Approach to Evaluation As If People Mattered*, Brighton: Institute of Development, University of Sussex.

Illich, I. (1981), *Shadow Work*, London: Marion Boyars.

Imboden, N. (1978), *A Management Approach to Project Appraisal and Evaluation*, Paris: OECD.

Marsden, D. (1990), *A Study of Officials: An Organisational Analysis of the Urban Community Development Department, Municipal Corporation of Hyderabad.* CDS Occasional Paper Series. Swansea: Centre for Development Studies, University College of Swansea.

Mcpherson, S. (1982), *Social Policy in the Third World: The Social Dilemmas of Underdevelopment,* Brighton: Harvester.

Merton, R.M. et al. (eds.) (1979), *Qualitative and Quantitative Social Research: Papers in Honour of Paul F. Lazarsfeld,* New York: Free Press.

Oakley, P. (1986), 'Evaluating social development', *Journal of Social Development in Africa,* No. 1.

Oakley, P. (1988), *The Monitoring and Evaluation of Participation in Rural Development,* Rome: FAO.

Parlett, M. and D. Hamilton (1972), *Evaluation as Illumination,* Edinburgh: University of Edinburgh Press.

Patton, M.Q. (1987), *How to Use Qualitative Methods in Evaluation,* London: Sage.

Rahman, M.A. (1983), *SARILAKAS: A Pilot Project for Stimulating Grassroots Participation in the Philippines,* Geneva: International Labour Organisation.

Rahman, M.A. (1986), personal field notes on visits to grassroots work in Bangladesh.

Rahman, M.A. (1987), personal field notes on visits to grassroots work in Bangladesh.

Rahman, M.A. (1989), *Glimpses of the 'Other Africa',* Geneva: International Labour Organisation.

Richards, H. (1985), *The Evaluation of Cultural Action,* Basingstoke: Macmillan.

Rondinelli, D.A. (1983), *Development Projects as Policy Experiments,* London: Methuen.

Rutman, L. (ed.) (1977), *Evaluation Research Methods,* London: Sage.

Sachs, I. (1987), *Development and Planning,* Cambridge: Cambridge University Press.

de Silva, G.V.S. et al. (1979), 'Bhoomi Sena: A struggle for people's power', *Development Dialogue,* No. 2.

Sutherland, A. (1989), *Sociology in Farming Systems Research,* London: Overseas Development Institute.

Tilakaratna, S. (1985), *The Animator in Participatory Rural Development: Some Experiences from Sri Lanka,* Geneva: International Labour Organisation.

Tripodi, T. et al. (1971), *Social Programme Evaluation,* University of Michigan Press.

United Nations (1984), *Guiding Principles for the Design and Use of M &
E in Rural Development Programmes*, Rome: UN.
Wade, R. (1982), 'The system of administrative and political corruption:
canal irrigation in South India', *Journal of Development Studies*, 18/3.
Weiss, C. (1972), *Evaluation Research*, New Jersey: Prentice Hall.
Wildavsky, A. (1979), *The Art and Craft of Policy Analysis*, Basingstoke:
Macmillan.
Wolfe, M. (1982), *Illusive Development*, Geneva: UNRISD.

List of conference participants

Patricia Aguilar-Albores, Institute of Development Studies, University of Sussex, UK
Ruth Alsop, School of Development Studies, University of East Anglia, UK
Iara Altafin, Emater/DF-Sain, Brasilia, Brazil
Helen Appleton, Intermediate Technology Development Group, Rugby, UK
Mark Attabeh, Archdiocesan Development Office, Tamale, Ghana
Judi Aubel, Pritech, Dakar, Senegal
Jan Bahnson-Jenson, DANIDA, Copenhagen, Denmark
Massy Bandera, Agricultural Extension and Rural Development Department, University of Reading, UK
Suraj Bandyopadhyay, Indian Statistical Institute, Calcutta, India
David Brown, Agricultural Extension and Rural Development Department, University of Reading, UK
Anne Buckley, Agricultural Extension and Rural Development Department, University of Reading, UK
Teresita Castillo, Presidential Management Staff, Manila, Philippines
Ann Conroy, Lilongwe, Malawi
Mauro da Costa Sousa, Ceris, Rio de Janeiro, Brazil
Gary Craig, York, UK
Genevieve de Crombrugghe, COTA (Collectif d'Echanges pour la Technologie Approprie*), Brussels, Belgium
Leith Dunn, Christian Aid, London, UK
Martin Dutting, Misereor, Aachen, Germany
Ralph Ec-Lumor, Project Planning Centre, University of Bradford, UK
Philippe Egger, International Labour Organisation, Geneva, Switzerland
Tony Fernandes, CEBEMO, Ab Oegstgeest, Netherlands
Marie-Therese Feuerstein, London, UK
Ignacio Garaycochea, ICD, Puna, Peru
Janice Giffen, Action Aid, London, UK
Patricia Goldey, Agricultural Extension and Rural Development Department, University of Reading, UK
Han de Groot, NOVIB, The Hague, Netherlands
Gabriel Guerrero, SEPADE (Servicio Evangelico para el Desarrollo), Santiago, Chile
Philip Harding, Overseas Development Administration, London, UK
Rip Hodson, Action Aid, London, UK
Helan Jaworsky, Rome, Italy

Haile Kahssay, World Health Organisation, Geneva, Switzerland
Volker Kasch, Association of the Church's Development Service, Stuttgart, Germany
Shakeeb Khan, Action Aid, London, UK
Stephen King, CAFOD, London, UK
Shadrak Kiungu, NCCK, Nairobi, Kenya ‣
Heinz-Bernd Knuvener, Misereor, Aachen, Germany
Ranjani Krishnamurthy, Institute of Development Studies, University of Sussex, UK
Nga-Huy Liem, CEMDHRRA (Centre for the Development of Human Resources in Rural Asia), Manila, Philippines
Andrew Lochhead, Swansea, Wales, UK
Hermione Lovell, Institute of Child Health, London, UK
Susan Lund, National Committee Against Removals, Cape Town, South Africa
John MacDonald, Department of Education, University of Manchester, UK
Gonzalo Martin Mandly, Instituto de Apoyo Agrario, Lima, Peru
Mellon Manyonga, Provincial Planning Unit, Ndola, Zambia
David Marsden, Centre for Development Studies, University College, Swansea, UK
Kathryn McPhail, World Bank, Washington, USA
Ruvimbo Mujene, NOVIB, Harare, Zimbabwe
Josphat Mulyungi, ISS, The Hague, Netherlands
Peter Oakley, Agricultural Extension and Rural Development Department, University of Reading
Tony O'Dwyer, APSO (Agency for Personal Service Overseas), Dublin, Ireland
Eugenia Piza Lopez, Oxfam, Oxford, UK
Brian Pratt, Oxfam, Oxford, UK
Aba Quainoo, Agricultural Extension and Rural Development Department, University of Reading, UK
Muhammad Anisur Rahman, International Labour Organisation, Geneva, Switzerland
Alan Rew, Centre for Development Studies, University College, Swansea, UK
Kate Robins, Action Aid, Nairobi, Kenya
Mark Robinson, Overseas Development Institute, London, UK
John Rouse, FAO, Rome, Italy
Frances Rubin, Oxfam, Oxford, UK
Md Shahabuddin, PROSHIKA, Dhaka, Bangladesh

Pablo Sidersky, Recife, Brazil
Trish Silkin, London, UK
Peter Sollis, Oxfam, Oxford, UK
Rajesh Tandon, New Delhi, India
Laurence Taylor, Selly Oak Colleges, Birmingham, UK
W.R. Temu, CORAT Africa (Christian Organizations Research and Advisory Trust of Africa), Nairobi, Kenya
Delle Tiongson-Brouwers, MASAI (Management Advancement System Association Inc), Quezon, Philippines
Pramod Unia, Oxfam, Oxford, UK
Norman Uphoff, RDC, Cornell University, USA
Tony van Zutphen, CEBEMO, Ab Oegstgeest, Netherlands
Laura Varga Vargas, Alforja, San Jose, Costa Rica
Koenraad Verhagen, CEBEMO, Ab Oegstgeest, Netherlands
Peter Wichmand, Action Aid, London, UK
Geoff Wood, Centre for Development Studies, University of Bath, UK